A PROTESTANT BAR MITZVAH

Raising Men and Women of Faith

Ladd C, Hoffman MD, MBA, MHA

Scripture quotations marked NIV are taken from the Holy Bible, New International Version ®, NIV ®. Copyright © 1973, 1978, 1984, 2011 by Biblica, Inc.™ Used by permission. All rights reserved worldwide. The "NIV" and "New International Version" are trademarks registered in the United States Patent and Trademark Office by Biblica, Inc.™.

Please note the pronouns of deity are often capitalized in honor of my mother, LouEllen Hoffman, as she would take the time in her Bible to capitalize any pronoun referring to Jesus.

Logo and the boy's rings were created by Jeweler Jay Phinney from The Karat Patch at 1003 E FM 700 in Big Spring, TX 79720. Phone (432) 267-1480.
https://www.thekaratpatch.com/

A Protestant Bar Mitzvah: Raising Men and Women of Faith
Copyright © 2023 by Ladd C. Hoffman MD, MBA, MHA

Final edit by Lincoln Crea Hoffman.

All Rights Reserved. No portion of this book may be used or reproduced in any form or by any electronic or mechanical means, including information storage and retrieval systems, without written permission in writing from the author, Stillwood Publishing or given publisher, except by reviewers, who may quote brief passages in a review.

ISBN: 978-1-961448-00-1 (Paperback Edition)

Visit www.AProtestantBarMitzvah.com
Cover Photography by Sam Smead
Visit www.Stillwood.estate

First Printing June 2023 / Printed in the United States of America

CONTENTS

Foreword v

Prelude 1
The Groundwork 3
Why Sixteen? 7
Why Piano or Violin? 11
Who Should Come? 16
Scripture at Beck and Call 20
Defense of Faith Part One 32
Defense of Faith Part Two 36
Defense of Faith Part Three 39
Defense of Faith Part Four 44
Defense of Faith Part Five 48
Defense of Faith Part Six 52
Defense of Faith Part Seven 56
Defense of Faith Part Eight 60
Passing the Baton of Faith 64
A Man Shares His Verses 68
A Man Leads a Prayer 72
Saturday Morning Came Without Warning 76
Mentor One 79
Mentor Two 85
Mentor Five 89
Mentor Four 94
Mentor Three 98
The Mentors Have Spoken, Let's Finish Strong 103
Unintended Side Effect 107
First Born Lincoln Crea Hoffman 110
Second Born Levi Cort Hoffman 114

Third Born Legend Cy Hoffman 117
Mentor LouEllen Hoffman 122
Mentor Carolyn T. Tipton 124
Mentor Daron Moore 127
Attendee Tucker Barraclough 133
Attendee Mark Lindsey 136
Attendee Sherry Lindsey 138
Attendee Jean Hodges 140
Attendee Dr. D. Ward 142
Attendees Elayne and Ernie Hanson 145
Postlude 149

About the author 151

FOREWORD

Recently, we finished our third and last Protestant Bar Mitzvah. Although we were never instructed on how to perform the process, we accomplished the goal. With a few examples, we made a plan. With no road map to follow, we found a way. <u>Even though I had never participated in a similar event in my life, we forged ahead.</u>

We did it!

Today, we set out to share with you what happened in the lives of the young men who stepped up, defended their faith, responded to queries, and presented their maturity.

We want you to experience the ups and downs of the process.

We want to challenge you to consider some type of ceremony or event for your offspring.

This book is dedicated to Lincoln, Levi, and Legend.

Young Men -   Never Quit!
              Never Give In!
              And always remember the hurdles are there to stop those who do not have the fiber to succeed.

I Believe in You!
You are my beloved sons, in whom I am well pleased.

Love,

Your Earthly Father.

PRELUDE

Through the pages of this text, you will see the following declaration:
Let's lay a stone here.

As we walk through the event of calling a young one to adulthood, may I share a verse from the Old Testament?

<u>1 Samuel 7:12 (NIV)</u>:
12 Then Samuel took a stone and set it up between Mizpah and Shen. He named it Ebenezer, saying, "Thus far the LORD has helped us."

You get to mark the significant moments of your life.
You get to decide what is important.
You get to name the life changing event.
You get to decide where and when to lay a stone.

No one tells you where, <u>you decide</u>. You decide when, where, how and why you call your child to reach adulthood.

My appreciation goes to many folks in my life. "Thank you" is kind of limited in expressing my gratitude:

The Mentors of Lincoln, Levi, and Legend.

My beloved, Rhonda.

My family.

My friends.

The call schedule that kept me at the hospital late at night to write.

Whoever reads this book and feels motivated to make a positive change for their little ones.

How do you declare a boy a Man?

How do you declare a girl a Woman?

How do you do something that was not done for you? Something you were never shown. Something you have not really even considered.

You follow the example of one who walked the path before you. You steal their ideas. You adapt it to your child. You make it your own.

You Decide.

THE GROUNDWORK

Decisions about having a child are complex.
We struggled with waiting until we were prepared.
We struggled with knowing if we could afford a child.
We struggled with the concept of bringing a soul into the world. We worried.

But 24 years ago, we were blessed by the birth of our firstborn son, Lincoln.

Weeks earlier, my Mother-In-Law had been awakened by a dream, clearly seeing a chubby 10-pound baby girl. She then awoke my Father-In-Law and told him about her dream and the beautiful little girl that she had seen in it.

On the scheduled day, since the baby's head was larger than the birth canal (Cephalopelvic Disproportion - C.P.D.), we had a set time to arrive at the hospital for my wife to undergo a Cesarean section. Until that moment, we had purposefully decided to remain uninformed of the gender of the baby; we were rather excited about the whole prospect. My one job of the day was to notify our audience of the results. Family and friends were gathered in the pre-celebration mode. Donuts were on the table.

Standing in the operating room gowned, gloved, hatted and glowing, I waited for the sounds of victory. First came the cry then came the proclamation, "Mr. And Mrs. Hoffman, you have a healthy baby boy."

As I carried our precious little one wrapped in soft cloth to the warmer, I turned to the window and our family and mouthed, "It's a boy!" with slightly raised eyebrows.

Then, he peed on me.

Although I could not hear the exchange on the other side of the glass, I was told that my Father-In-Law turned to my Mother-In-Law and said, "Don't you ever wake me up again to tell me your dreams!" How I wish that video could have been taken of the exchange.

And so, the journey began.

Lincoln Crea became my go-to focus of attention. In reality, he had been a focus for months prior. We had often read to an ever-growing uterus. We played music and discussed which type of sounds caused the most stimulation in this growing gift. We had prayed for, hoped for, saved for, and waited for this little one.

As a blessing, I worked nights while my beloved worked days. So, 'Mr. Mom' was not totally out of the realm of titles for me. My Aunt can tell you of when I jogged to her insurance office with Lincoln in a shoulder strap backpack, sound asleep. We cruised the neighborhood in a trike carrier with a safety strap that I kept around my wrist as I jogged. We worked puzzles, read books, listened to talk radio, and ate homemade food that my wife would blend and freeze in ice trays for almost perfect sized servings that just needed to be heated up.

Then an idea began to form:

Someday, Lincoln would be a man.

Without knowing much more than at some time in the future,

this young one would stand as a man, I began to tell him that a day was coming when I would expect him to be a man. This day would be significant. This day would be life changing. This day would be memorable. This day would be specifically dedicated to him. This day would be marked on the calendar of his life. This day would change my perception of him. This day would be declared to the world. There would be no going back.

Honestly, I had no idea what much of that meant, but you could see in his eyes that he got the significance of something BIG coming on the horizon.

This message was reinforced purposefully. Throughout his childhood, you could ask Lincoln about what was coming, and he would tell you about the coming day of Manhood.

So, if you need a starting place, Let's lay a stone here and say that every young man and woman needs to be informed of your expectations concerning their maturity. Clearly stating that a day is coming when they will be considered an adult gives a focal point to guide, a center point to aim, a high point to reach, and a map point to direct.

For if there is never a focal point to guide, there may be too many years of aimless wondering. If there never is a center point to aim, the shots of life will most assuredly be off target. If there is never a high point to reach, the outstretched arm will never be challenged. And if there is never a map point to direct, the young ones can be easily led astray.

What if this story has come to you later in life, and you feel that you missed your opportunity to lay the groundwork for this plan? Start today. Start where you are. Pick out some of the ideas in the coming pages. Throw away the ones that will not work. Create your own. Create a strategy that reflects the value you place on your child.

Write it down. You might be able to share what you created and the outcomes you achieved with me one day.

I had never seen a coming-of-age ceremony. I had never written a program for a ceremony. I had never completed a ceremony, until a weekend in March, 16 years after the birth of our firstborn son.

You have been blessed with a child or children.
You have invested in their lives.
Your child will one day be an adult.
You will tell your child about the coming day.
You will grow the expectations and plans.
Everyone will know your plans.
See it to the end.

WHY SIXTEEN?

Why did I choose 16 years old?

When I operate on a patient, the question always arises: "When do you want to see me back in the office?"

So, a decision had to be made. One week concerned me about the possibility of being too close to surgery and not truly having recovered from the 'assault.' Three weeks seemed a little like I didn't care, and I was shooting for a post-operative billing charge that might fall outside of the global billing reimbursement period. Two weeks became my line in the sand. Interestingly, some physicians never see a patient post-operatively, and have a Nurse Practitioner or a Physician Assistant do the follow up visits for them. I decided on two weeks.

I could be wrong or could be right. Who knows? But I needed a number to fill the blank space on the post-operative orders. I chose two weeks since most patients are almost fully recovered by that time, and I had an answer every single time that question arose without exerting much effort. Yes, there are exceptions, some folks concern me so much that I schedule their follow up in a few days, and some actually never show up for their follow up appointment.

So, how did I choose 16 years old for my line of demarcation?

My Jewish friends chose 13 for the boys and 12 for the girls. My Hispanic friends chose 15 for the girls but cloudier for the boys. The Government chose 18 for voting and registering for Selective Service.

There was and is no perfect number. No perfect point in time. My thoughts centered on my boys opening the door of driving without an adult in the front seat. As the world opened, my heart led me to hope that my young ones would also be opening themselves to the rights, responsibilities, and expectations of being a man.

Is the decision as simple as scratching a line in the sand?

Let's ask the opposite question. What if you never declare a time of maturity?

You should expect a continual haze of uncertainty to be present in your child. There will never be a moment when they were expected to pick up the gauntlet and to accept the challenge of adult living. They will be skating along in the whimsical freedom of low expectations.

They would not have to balance a checkbook. They would not have to pray in public, speak in public, answer in public, or lead in public. They would not have to be responsible for siblings who might ride in the vehicle under their leadership and decisions.

Simply, never setting a definitive number allows enough wiggle room for the tires of life to fall off the axle of reality.

Alternatively, you have provided yourself with a bit of grace and freedom by placing a definitive mark. You will have an answer. The goal is set. The standard is defined. The expectations are clear. You can take a deep breath.

Will your little one be ready for the date that you have set?

I worried about that question quite a lot. To me, it appears that my anxiety revolved more around my efforts to equip the boy than upon his state of readiness. Setting a goal propels you on the path to ready your child for what is coming. My dreams would arouse me in the morning to pray for the boys. An unsettled spirit would make me re-evaluate my decisions about the verses chosen for them to memorize. I would rewrite sections of the ceremony after second-guessing my motives. The mentors that I had chosen would turn me down for spring break commitments, actual speaking engagements (my old Sunday School Teacher), and even a tennis tournament. The mentors that survived to the end were prayed over multiple times in order from first to last, (Sorry Daron, you were 5th and many times I got distracted prior to finishing the list).

Yet, the ball was already rolling. It started rolling years prior when I told Lincoln that a day was coming.

Each book that I read in preparation was distilled to quality drops. I stole ideas from them and created my own. I researched the Jewish significance of Bar Mitzvahs. While teaching Sunday School, a thought would hit me of an obvious omission that needed to be corrected, and I would scribble it into my notebook, draw a box, and plan to make it better.

Is there an exact age that is always optimum? No.

You should be encouraged here. I did not know how to do this thing that resembled a Protestant Bar Mitzvah. At this moment in time, you may not either. In the coming pages, you will see some ideas. You will think creative thoughts. You will have a chance to plan.

So, pick a time, an age, and a goal. Let's lay a stone here.

What if you think that the time has passed? Who is to say that you cannot declare tomorrow the day? You can call upon your child to think of themselves differently. You can call upon yourself to think differently of them. If you ask them to memorize one verse a week, they will have 26 verses in their memory within half a year.

I chose 16, because I needed to make a decision and stick with it.

Also, at 16, the boys would still be under my roof, at least for a while, and I could help them navigate some mistakes and flubs that will undoubtedly happen in life. I am guaranteed to have tribulation in this world (John 16:33).

> You have been blessed with a child or children.
> You get to pick their age of maturity.
> You get to set the goal.
> You will never regret making a decision and sticking with it.
> You might regret not making a decision.
> Everyone can question and second-guess your decisions, but you are the one scratching the line in the sand.
> See it to the end.

WHY PIANO OR VIOLIN?

In my youth, my piano teacher came to the house, gave me some pointers, showed me some theory, asked me to write a report on a composer, and then opened her portable ashtray for her cigarette to sit on my Mom's piano.

Needless to say, my piano career came to an end.

It seems that I never fully recovered from that experience. Although mathematically, I could sit down and make any major chord, something happened at that event. Yes, I would play the trumpet in the Middle School Band, but piano never resurfaced from the tide of my life.

My Beloved played extensively. Her piano teacher is still living. She was disciplined with practice and performance. She also played the flute, sang in choirs and ensembles, and she had a scholarship to play trumpet in the band at her university.

So, what do you do for your progeny?

My Beloved began our little ones in the Suzuki Method of piano and violin when they were 5 or 6 years old. You see, Shin'ichi Suzuki believed kids should learn music like they learn a language. They copy the sounds they hear first, then learn the letters, words, reading, and formal grammar later.

So, our home and cars have had Suzuki music playing in the background for years.

Sure Ladd, you started years ago, but you may ask, "What about me? We wanted to do music lessons, but never had the time, energy, or money."

I will confess to you, that I did not pick piano or violin for my sons. Actually, due to my life experience, I probably had a twinge of dislike for the piano. As a way of self-protection from my piano failure, I assigned an effeminate quality to the instrument and steered clear.

But what about your little one?

If you see a need for music, then please commit and hold fast. Don't quit. Endure. Find an answer when the child sits with arms crossed, frowning, and does not want to practice.

Levi (our Number 2!) was sitting on the couch with a glare in his eyes. Piano practice was no fun. He did not want to do it. No one was going to make him do it. Nothing was going to change his mind.

So, I sat down.

Looked him in the glare and said, "You know Levi, we should find some way to link your piano playing to a video game. If you played well, the bombs would go off.

EXPLOSIONS would jump at 40% of the completed piece.

MACHINE GUNS would spray at 50%.

TANKS would move at 70%.

ROCKETS, MAYHEM, Oh, the humanity of it all!"

I went to the kitchen, but there was a glimmer in the last recesses of his eyes.

Then I heard a familiar piece methodically being practiced. I ran to the end of the piano and started to jump up and down like an idiot. I made noises the best I could of explosions, destruction, machine guns, and bazookas. My animation was really embarrassing.

But Levi was laughing.

He was actually crying with laughter. And He was practicing.

Within 5 minutes, he had gone from arms crossed in defiance to a smiling young one practicing his music.

To this day, if I hear him practicing and am near the piano, I can still make him smile and sometimes laugh out loud.

You can find a way. I'm not that facile at child psychology to have come up with that solution all by myself. Thank you, LORD!

So why piano? My Beloved believed that the life lessons of practice, listening, playing, learning, and performing were really beyond measure in value.

I went to work.

Lincoln played.

Levi played.

Legend played.

I praised.

While exploring a hospital many years ago for a possible position, we found a dusty piano in the cafeteria. I approached the most in-charge person I could find and asked if my children could play the instrument. After a kind of concerned scan from head to toe, we were given permission, Mr. Suzuki proposed that you should only practice on the days that you eat. So, when we occasionally got ourselves into a bind, I became a kind of Fixer/Solver for the daily piano requirement.

Lincoln sat down and began playing. Levi played next. The cafeteria manager smiled. In a moment he brought out a small bowl, placed it on top of the piano, and put a few coins inside. The cadre of regulars drinking coffee got the clue and followed suit. We have those coins in a boxed frame with a note clearly indicating the significance of the first money the boys ever earned playing the piano.

You see, where I got an ashtray and a cigarette, my sons got some spare change as a tip!

Clearly, the trajectory of my life does not need to decide, limit, or block the trajectory of my children.

Let's lay a stone here.

While traveling once, I found a piano in the main ballroom of our resort. I approached the front desk and inquired about the boys practicing. The idea was summarily rejected. Undeterred, I asked the following question, "How much to rent the piano for an hour?" This pushed the issue above the pay grade of the front desk staff and the manager was summoned to address the issue. As politely as possible, I again asked about the piano and made it very clear that I was willing to pay for the use of the instrument for an hour (Fixer/Solver of the daily piano ticket!).

Clearly the manager was tussling with "the customer is always right" principle. After a moment, she stated that we could use the piano, followed us through the door and quickly shut it behind us to protect the other guests from the coming storm.

Piano practice began and a funny thing happened. As the polished pieces began to waft melodically through the ballroom, someone at the front desk came and opened the doors wide and fixed them so they would not close. People walking by stopped and looked. Mommy and Daddy glowed from the sweat equity of driving to lessons, paying for lessons, practicing pieces, listening to Suzuki music, encouraging discouraged little ones, competing at piano competitions, pleading with stubborn boys, and maintaining the goal.

Friday night would be marked as a "Piano Recital and Coming of Age Celebration" or "Violin Recital and Coming of Age Celebration."

Piano and violin were chosen to start the ceremonies, because these were a part of the boys' lives. In reality, music is woven into the fabric of each of them. As we have traveled, we have played in hotels. We rode in a cab to a music store on the other side of town to get practice accomplished. We've played in a bar during the day and the patrons did not mind (the only place I could find a piano!). Lincoln once played on a concert grand piano that cost more than my first 2 houses (I had offered to rent it, but they also allowed us to use it for no charge).

So, what quality, activity, interest, sport, or characteristic is specific for your little one? You can start with that special thing, or you can skip this part and focus on the task at hand.

The boys all played the pieces that they had selected. They spoke before each piece about the significance of the music and what they wanted the audience to hear. That aspect of the ceremony made it special for them. This also required me to get a piano tuner to the Ballroom before the event to ensure a good tone!

You can find a way to make it special for your future man or woman.

Recently, Legend played a gig in Colorado, where he attends college. Rhonda, my Mother-In-Law (dreamer!), and my mother went to support him. One of the best lines from the event was when my Mother-In-Law said, "I have never been to a bar on a Sunday." She had never been to a bar before and this restaurant had a stage with drinks being served, but Grandmother's love was great!

You have been blessed with a child or children.
You decide if music is a path you would like to go down.
You decide what special interest your child might like
    to share.
You decide how to invest your sweat equity.
You decide who would like to see this aspect of your child.
Everyone can disagree with your choice.
See it to the end.

WHO SHOULD COME?

So, how large should the event be?

We lived in a rather small town. After the closure of a training base for pilots many years ago, the town dwindled down. Most of the people in town have either heard about you, met you, know your family, or crossed paths with you through work, church, grocery store, or restaurants.

When deciding how to tell folks about the event, I was still in the old school modes of communication: radio, newspaper, and church bulletin.

It may seem hard to believe, but I have never had any presence on any social media platform. Never have I seen a post from someone else, so this avenue was not even an option for me.

To start with, I went to our church and asked if a notice could be placed in the bulletin to invite our church family to the event. Many of these folks knew the boys, Rhonda and I, and some even worked at the hospital with me.

The local newspaper had experienced the same decline that affected all print media over the years, but I was acquainted with one of the account executives who had previously requested my support for advertising campaigns.

After a little back and forth, the following Ad was written and submitted to the paper:

> Piano Recital & Coming of Age Celebration
> Friday ~ 7:00 pm
> March 13th
> Historic Hotel Settles
> Mezzanine and Grand Ballroom
> Featuring:
> Lincoln Crea Hoffman
> Piano / Scripture / Defense of Faith
> Passing of Baton

Since I had previously been interviewed at the local radio station at the behest of the hospital's marketing director when we arrived in town, I decided to go back and ask about cutting a radio ad. Most stations have requirements for public service announcement quotas, but I was willing to pay for a personal ad to get the job done. They agreed without much fuss, and my sons got to tour the radio station, and got to see an entire program being broadcast from a computer processing syndicated feeds of national programs. This ended up being a great learning experience for the boys.

We wrote a script for a 30 second ad. Since I had never written a script before, let alone a time-constrained one, we had some fun. We needed some background music, so the boys recorded portions of their favorite recital piece and we brought the audio file with us to the station. The engineer set us up in a recording booth, gave us a countdown, and we acted out our script:

After a few seconds of music intro.

>Me: Hey Lincoln, that's some pretty good piano music.
>Lincoln: Yes sir, it is. And you can hear more.
>Me: When?
>Lincoln: Friday Night, March 13th at 7:00 pm.
>Me: Where's that?
>Lincoln: Historic Hotel Settles Grand Ballroom, 200 East 3rd Street in Downtown Big Spring.
>Me: A piano recital?
>Lincoln: A recital, and a coming-of-age celebration for me.
>Me: So, you're going to defend your faith in front of God and everyone?
>Lincoln: Yes sir, I will.
>Me: How much does it cost?
>Lincoln: Dad, we are going to melt your credit card!
>Me: Friday, March 13th, 7:00 pm, Hotel Settles Grand Ballroom.
>Lincoln: Dad, can I have the keys to the truck now?

The radio engineer made us sound like professionals.

One day while on the elliptical at lunch time, I heard our ad on KBST 1490 AM playing during the most listened to radio talk show (Rush Limbaugh). I called Rhonda and shared a little bit of my excitement. Some staff at work commented on my melting credit card. One friend at church asked if I had my truck keys in my pocket.

The message got out.

My value for the event is reflected by the preparation.

I wanted all of the boys to know what was happening. This was not a time for privacy. Let's lay a stone here. This was open to the world.

Come if you want to see a young one advance into adulthood.

You may or may not want to go this far. Remember, I overdid this thing. But you can determine how many others to invite and to share this moment with. In today's world, social media may be an avenue of promotion.

We varied the script slightly for each kid, the advertisements had different dates, and the names changed each time, but we walked this road for 3 young men.

You have been blessed with a child or children.
You decide who you would like to attend.
You decide how you would like to invite others.
You decide what creative needs you might require to
    accomplish this.
You decide how hard you want to swing for the fence.
Everyone can say that you are going overboard.
See it to the end.

SCRIPTURE AT BECK AND CALL

If you were to attend one of my Sunday School classes over the years, you would see the following proclamation on the first few slides of the lesson (slight variation of the NIV version of Scripture):

2 Timothy 3:16 This is my Bible, it is inspired by God and it is profitable for teaching, for reproof, for correcting and for training in righteousness,

Psalm 119:105 It is a lamp unto my feet and a light unto my path.

Psalm 119:11 I have hidden It in my heart that I might not sin against You.

What better starting point than Scripture?

This was a foundational principle that I longed for my sons to understand. They needed to have Scripture ready at their mental fingertips. The need to have the melody of verses playing in the background of their lives, much like the Suzuki Music had played in the cars and rooms of our lives. They needed to be able to quote it from memory, and I even wanted them to know the references for the verses.

Is that too much to ask?

How high do they set the bar for Olympic Athletes? High enough to win the prize.

Yes, I could have told him not to worry about the references. I could have lowered the bar of expectation on the number of verses. I could have lessened the load of questions that they needed to be prepared to answer. I could have done many things that would have decreased the value of the Gold Medal at the end of the competition (or the gold ring in this case).

Bluntly, my fears, weaknesses, and failures as a father should not be transferred to the possibilities that lay before these young men. We often make concessions based on our own limitations. So, the die was cast. The decisions were made. The verses were chosen.

Did I choose the perfect verses for all of life's lessons?

Did I cover every single thing that would present itself as a life hurdle before them?

Did I address every temptation that would befall them?

No.

No.

And No.

What I did was to review my life experiences. In retrospect, there were certain significant events in my life that stood out above the rest due to the profound impact they had on me. More clearly, the craters they left after the meteorite had struck the foundation of my being. I knew the time of construction would be months in length, so I devised an 8-week staging plan with weekly assignments for the boys to complete before the ceremony to allow them to internalize the necessary skills and knowledge within the given timeframe.

Week One:

On one occasion, when opening my door, a young man in a white shirt with a thin black tie and a name badge that said, "Elder" greeted me with a smile. We exchanged pleasantries. He opened his scripture to John 1:1 and read, "In the beginning was the word, and the word was with god, and the word was a god."

The alarm bells went off, and my mind raced through the Scripture that I had memorized. So naturally, these Scriptures became the starting point for the boys.

John 1:1-7 (NIV):

1 In the beginning was the Word, and the Word was with God, and the Word was God.

2 He was with God in the beginning.

3 Through Him all things were made; without Him nothing was made that has been made.

4 In Him was life, and that life was the light of all mankind.

5 The light shines in the darkness, and the darkness has not overcome it.

6 There was a man sent from God whose name was John.

7 He came as a witness to testify concerning that light, so that through Him all might believe.

The boys needed to know that the Deity of Jesus should not to be diminished by an indefinite article, "a." They needed to know that others would alter their scripture. They needed to be facile in wielding the blade of scriptura (Latin).

These verses led to the next obvious question, "If John came to testify about the light so that all men might believe through Jesus, how can I be saved?

Romans 10:9-10 (NIV):

9 If you declare with your mouth, "Jesus is Lord," and believe in your heart that God raised Him from the dead, you will be saved.

10 For it is with your heart that you believe and are justified, and it is with your mouth that you profess your faith and are saved.

Week One held both the foundation of Jesus and the salvation through Jesus. Nine verses for the first week with the references. These verses are extremely important to me. My sons would need to know them for their celebration.

Week Two:

At 16 years of age, you might be slightly intimidated by the prospect of speaking about Christ. That thought reminded me of a sermon I had the opportunity to deliver many years ago. So most assuredly the boys would need to know how to respond when the accuser hissed that they were too young to speak about Jesus.

Jeremiah 1:6-8 (NIV):

6 "Alas, Sovereign LORD," I said, "I do not know how to speak; I am too young."

7 But the LORD said to me, "Do not say, 'I am too young.' You must go to everyone I send you to and say whatever I command you.

8 Do not be afraid of them, for I am with you and will rescue you," declares the LORD.

My deepest heart desire is that my sons will be able to speak to anyone, anywhere, and on any day about Christ. But what if someone speaks harshly about your faith, your Bible, your church, or your Savior?

Ezekiel 2:6-7 (NIV):

6 And you, son of man, do not be afraid of them or their words. Do not be afraid, though briers and thorns are all around you and you live among scorpions. Do not be afraid of what they say or be terrified by them, though they are a rebellious people.

7 You must speak My words to them, whether they listen or fail to listen, for they are rebellious.

At this point in front of many in the audience, I told my sons of my yearning for them to never be afraid. It was not an empty quest. Preparation, dedication, education, and expectation can help dispel fear.

Week two dispelled youth as an excuse and fear of man as a limiter.

Week Three:

Do the boys have any promise about their ability to pray to an Infinite God?

Jeremiah 33:2-3 (NIV):

2 "This is what the LORD says, He who made the earth, the LORD who formed it and established it—the LORD is His name:

3 'Call to Me and I will answer you and tell you great and unsearchable things you do not know.'

Please know that the Lord Himself has instructed you to call upon Him. But what if you find yourself worrying about the stuff of this life: the job, classes, relationships, finances, or health issues?

Philippians 4:6-7 (NIV):

6 Do not be anxious about anything, but in every situation, by prayer and petition, with thanksgiving, present your requests to God.

7 And the peace of God, which transcends all understanding, will guard your hearts and your minds in Christ Jesus.

There is no way I can describe the peace of God to the boys. They must experience it for themselves. You must experience it for yourself.

Week Three called the boys to pray and called them to peace through prayer.

Week Four:

When you go to school, your biology 101 professors will tell you that you evolved from a primordial soup, with random mutations, spiced with millions of years, and driven by energy from the sun. What foundation can you stand upon? Understand, I have spent years on this issue with my sons. They know to expect merciless attacks upon this point.

Genesis 1:1-3 (NIV):

1 In the beginning God created the heavens and the earth.

2 Now the earth was formless and empty, darkness was over the surface of the deep, and the Spirit of God was hovering over the waters.

3 And God said, "Let there be light," and there was light.

When Richard Dawkins, author of The God Delusion, was asked by Ben Stein in the movie "Expelled: No Intelligence Allowed" how did the first self-replicating molecule happen and where it came from, Richard responded, from "A higher intelligence from elsewhere in the universe." You see, Richard can believe in aliens, but my sons cannot believe in The Creator. So, I asked the boys to get a reference point for the "wise men" like Dawkins.

1 Corinthians 1:18-20 (NIV):

18 For the message of the cross is foolishness to those who are perishing, but to us who are being saved it is the power of God.

19 For it is written: "I will destroy the wisdom of the wise; the intelligence of the intelligent I will frustrate."

20 Where is the wise person? Where is the teacher of the law? Where is the philosopher of this age? Has not God made foolish the wisdom of the world?

In my lifetime, I have been told of a coming Ice Age (Walter Cronkite on September 11, 1972), a coming Melting Age (Al Gore), and a coming Climate Changing Age (current fear mongering term). Since I made it through the 70s and 80s, I know that we did not freeze. The hockey stick has been disproven. I have been told that the sea level will rise and Floridians will be swimming: (Now, consider Jeremiah 5:22 (NIV) "Should you not fear Me?' declares the LORD. 'Should you not tremble in My presence? I made the sand a boundary for the sea, an everlasting barrier it cannot cross. The waves may roll, but they cannot prevail; they may roar, but they cannot cross it.") I watched a house committee hearing where "experts" were asked what percentage of the atmosphere is carbon dioxide (CO_2)? The answers started at 5% and rose to 8%. You see, even the experts are making decisions about fossil fuels unaware that CO_2 is 0.04% of the atmosphere. It is a sad state of affairs.

Week four placed God as Creator and man as the decider about the message of the cross.

Week Five:

What if the struggle of life gets too hard for you, the expectation, the rules, or the hoops that you must jump through?

Isaiah 40:28-31 (NIV):

28 Do you not know? Have you not heard? The LORD is the everlasting God, the Creator of the ends of the earth. He will not grow tired or weary, and His understanding no one can fathom.

29 He gives strength to the weary and increases the power of the weak.

30 Even youths grow tired and weary, and young men stumble and fall;

31 but those who hope in the LORD will renew their strength. They will soar on wings like eagles; they will run and not grow weary; they will walk and not be faint.

The boys may grow tired and weary, but I want them to hope in the Lord. Your strength will be renewed. So, what about the temptations of this world, for they are many? They are strong. They will come.

1 Corinthians 10:12-13(NIV):

12 So, if you think you are standing firm, be careful that you don't fall!

13 No temptation has overtaken you except what is common to mankind. And God is faithful; He will not let you be tempted beyond what you can bear. But when you are tempted, he will also provide a way out so that you can endure it.

One of the ways out is to not be in the place of demise in the first place. After 24 years of haunting Emergency Rooms and responding to pages (there used to be things called pagers!), what have I told my sons? "Nothing good happens after midnight!" So, one of the ways out is to be asleep in your bed. Remember that.

Week five gives the boys a focus on hope (The Lord) and a promise of a way to escape temptation.

Week Six:
Say you mess up. Say you fail. Can you lose your salvation?

Romans 8:38-39 (NIV):
38 For I am convinced that neither death nor life, neither angels nor demons, neither the present nor the future, nor any powers,
39 neither height nor depth, nor anything else in all creation, will be able to separate us from the love of God that is in Christ Jesus our Lord.

Remember that you cannot be separated from the love of God that is in Christ Jesus. So, how do you live this life in the mess of the world that we have made?

Galatians 2:20 (NIV):
20 I have been crucified with Christ and I no longer live, but Christ lives in me. The life I now live in the body, I live by faith in the Son of God, who loved me and gave Himself for me.

Please know that you will live by faith in the Son of God.
Week six assures the boys of the inability of anything to remove God's love for them and the manifest presence of His living through them.

Week Seven:
But wait, you made a mistake, doesn't that disqualify you? Aren't you out of the race?

Ecclesiastes 7:20 (NIV):
20 Indeed, there is no one on earth who is righteous, no one who does what is right and never sins.

Boys, there is not a single person on this earth without sin. Are you certain about that?

Romans 3:22-23 (NIV):
22 This righteousness is given through faith in Jesus Christ to all who believe. There is no difference between Jew and Gentile,
23 for all have sinned and fall short of the glory of God,

The certainty that I want you to remember is that we are all in need of a Savior, because we are all sinners. There is not a single prayer being voiced today anywhere on this earth that is not coming from the lips or mind of a sinner.

Week Seven provides absolute certainty about the need for a Savior, as every single man and woman has sinned.

Week Eight:
Do you need to be careful about your faith?

2 John 1:8-9 (NIV):
8 Watch out that you do not lose what we have worked for, but that you may be rewarded fully.
9 Anyone who runs ahead and does not continue in the teaching of Christ does not have God; whoever continues in the teaching has both the Father and the Son.

Remember, that I want you to continue in the teachings of Christ, for then you will have the Father and the Son.

So, how do you possibly love others in this world?

1 John 4:10-11 (NIV):
10 This is love: not that we loved God, but that He loved us and sent His Son as an atoning sacrifice for our sins.

11 Dear friends, since God so loved us, we also ought to love one another.

Boys, please keep love for others as a part of your fiber, for your Heavenly Father and your earthly Mother and Father also love you.

Week eight reminds you to continue in the teaching of the One who loved you and sent His Son for you.

Starting 9 weeks before the ceremonies, I gave the boys the verses for the week. We practiced each night and reviewed the previous weeks. We looked ahead to the coming weeks, and we talked about the Why? of the verses. We rehearsed their responses to a question that would introduce each set of verses. We built a foundation of Scripture.

It is worth noting that many of these sessions were conducted over the phone. My job keeps me at the beck and call of the Emergency Room, the Surgical Floor, the Transfer Center, and previous patients. Many nights at the hospital, I cherished a moment to call home and ask my sons to grab their folders, while I sat with my folder, and we worked over the verses, the questions, and their development.

You will have to overcome hurdles while you work out the kinks of your child's ceremony. The possible hurdles are beyond even your wildest imagination. Easy does not apply. Simple is for others. Quick is a vapor. When you start, be committed to finishing. Let's lay a stone here.

Will 40 verses change your child? Will 30, 20, or 50?

In the weeks leading up to the rite, one of my sons told me of a class he was taking at school where he quoted one of the earlier Scriptures as a question response. I would love to tell you that I am that good at picking verses, but the Scripture can stand on its own merit.

There are great verses that I missed. There are theological issues that we did not address. There are glaring holes in our preparation. But we made the preparation.

Get a piece of paper and start listing the verses you believe are crucial for your child to live by.

You have been blessed with a child or children.
You decide what Scripture to memorize.
You decide what life events to address.
You decide how to tie the verses together.
You decide why some verses are so important to you.
Everyone can have different verses or reasons.
See it to the end.

DEFENSE OF FAITH
PART ONE

After the 40 verses of Scripture, I informed the audience that we were moving to a slightly different time. This segment would be open ended responses from the boys over eight questions. This would be a Defense of Faith. This would test them to stand strong when the attacks of life come on all fronts. The responses of the young men here would be evidence of their preparation.

First Question: Can you share with us your testimony?

My recollection clearly holds the gold stars of Scripture memory from First Baptist Church Heights. I remember the musty Sunday School classrooms. I remember T. McKenzie teaching my Sunday School class at First Baptist Church Houston. I remember my decision of faith in Jesus. Pastor John Bisagno baptized me at 12 years of age at FBC Houston. Nothing can take those memories from me.

The boys would need to be clear about their testimony.

When we started preparing for the ceremony, I posed the above question to each of the boys.

They recalled asking about sin, Jesus, and forgiveness. They spoke about praying to accept Jesus as Savior. Lincoln remembers his Baptism at Crossroads Baptist Church in San Antonio, Texas when he was 6 years old.

I reminded Lincoln that when he was about to be baptized, I asked Brother Doug to speak briefly, and while standing on the altar, looking up at him in the baptismal, I said to him, "Lincoln, you are my beloved son, in whom I am well pleased." I got to repeat this line at Levi's baptism, and to share these words with the congregation while I was baptizing Legend at First Baptist Church, Big Spring, Texas.

Were the boys ready to share these historical events with the world?

Not really.

First, I had them write out what they would say in response to the question. Then, I had them share it with their mother and me. Next, we had them re-write what they wanted to say. They practiced several times until they could respond without stumbling. Many of the courses on evangelism have this as a prerequisite to moving to the next phase of sharing your faith.

A 16-year-old is no different. They need to be prepared to share their testimony without fear and worry.

This is not an easy task. It takes thought. It takes the evaluation of phrases. It takes clarifying the where, when, how, what, and why of the change in your life.

I have given my testimony many times in my life. There is no fear in me relating to this issue. Time and practice have stamped out the embers of emotion.

How do I give confidence to my sons? Do I want that definitive conviction available to them at all times? Absolutely!

The only way to get there is to practice, practice, and practice.

Since we had 8 weeks of preparation and one week of review, the boys had 63 days to speak their testimony out loud in practice. What verse have you recited 63 days in a row. Do you remember it?

If piano takes years of rudimentary emphasis on every note to gracefully deliver the entire concept, how is giving away the story of your salvation different?

When Lincoln was 4 years old, he began to ask about being saved, and I was skeptical that he could understand the significance (His mother was more brilliant than I!).

Matthew 19:14 (NIV):
14 Jesus said, "Let the little children come to me, and do not hinder them, for the kingdom of heaven belongs to such as these."

My education, maturity, and knowledge are insufficient to block the path of one coming to Christ.

How do you get your child comfortable with this aspect of faith living?

You ask them.

You take it upon yourself to prepare them to stand firm.

You do your job.

If you wonder about this topic with your son or daughter, put this book down, call your gift from God to visit with you and just ask them.

Let's lay a stone here.

After preparing one night, we stopped for what I like to call, "Asking the Next Question."

Looking my firstborn in the eye, I asked, "Lincoln, can anyone ever take this away from you?"

"No sir."
Testimony is personal.
Testimony is strong.
Testimony changes lives.

You decide what questions to ask.
You decide how well prepared you want your child to be.
You decide what mechanism of practice works for you and them.
You decide when you feel confident in their response.
You decide if you need to address the missing structure in their faith.
Everyone has a testimony, whether good or bad.
See it to the end.

DEFENSE OF FAITH
PART TWO

Lincoln had given his testimony. He was succinct. He was clear. He got a jab in about his Dad thinking he was too young to make a decision, and his mother being smarter!

This was a great place to start, because the next question in front of 70 people could cause a little more consternation.

Second Question: What if someone says that your Scripture is not valid?

When reading Seeking Allah, Finding Jesus: A Devout Muslim Encounters Christianity, by Nabeel Qureshi, I was awakened again to the scriptural validity argument. How could someone outside of the Christian Faith, who does not love the Bible or who has never read the Bible approach this topic?

Time.

Data.

Research.

Nabeel had seen fit to seek information from another author: Josh McDowell (The New Evidence That Demands a Verdict:

Evidence I & II Fully Updated in One Volume To Answer the Questions Challenging Christians in the 21st Century).

Although certainty about Scripture propelled me to memorize, quote, teach, preach, and sing the Word of God, my certainty was not Lincoln's, Levi's, or Legend's certainty.

They would encounter challenging naysayers in their lives that would attack them on this point. It became vitally apparent that they needed to delve into this morass and come up swinging.

We started with Josh McDowell. We focused on specific chapters. We talked through the data. We talked through the implications. We looked closely at the three tests applied to the Bible: 1) Bibliographic test, 2) Internal Evidence test, and 3) External Evidence test.

Since I could not take Lincoln, Levi, or Legend back to my childhood and the small wooden plaque that hung on the wall above my bed:

Psalm 119:105 (NIV):
105 Your word is a lamp for my feet, a light on my path.

The need for them to establish the power of Scripture was forefront.

Yes, they had quoted 40 verses. Yes, they were going to share some of their favorite verses later in the program. Yes, they had prepared many verses for AWANA (Approved Workers Are Not Ashamed - 2 Timothy 2:15) through their youth.

Would that equip them for an assault against the validity of their Scripture?

How strong will the construction be when the real earthquake happens? The engineering diagrams will provide tolerances. The historical data will provide references with the highest and lowest data points. The cement will be graded for its pounds per square inch compression strength. Yet, none of these things will matter unless the building stands under the force of the attack.

We worked.

We worked more.

We worked some more.

A second time of emphasizing the soundness of research on the historicity of Scripture. An example from the next week where papyrus from the inside of a mask in an Egyptian tomb had verses from the gospel of Mark.

Brick by brick, we built.

As the ceremonies approached, the confidence had accrued.

What will you give to your child to face this attack? Just believe it?! That's the way it has always been?! I don't know?!

If this question causes you some concern, then please get busy and look deep. You will be able to teach and give away that which you know. So stand firm to the attack about validity.

Let's lay a stone here.

You decide the validity of your Scripture.
You decide how to convey that message.
You decide what sources to review.
You decide what counselors to reach out to for support.
You decide how strong the foundation you want to build.
Everyone may say this is too difficult of a task.
See it to the end.

DEFENSE OF FAITH
PART THREE

Bibliographically, internally, and externally Scripture stands strong. So the next punch would come from rejecting Jesus. Is He really who He claims to be? Did He really exist upon the stage of history? If a person rejects Him, then none of this other stuff really matters.

Third Question: Did Jesus Even Exist?

How many other humans changed the calendar?
B.C. - Before Christ
A.D. - Anno Domini (the year of our Lord).

Yes, I understand the movement to remove Jesus from the calendar:
B.C.E. - Before Common Era.
C.E. - Common Era.

But what made the change from B.C.E. to C.E.? The man Jesus made the change. The life of Jesus. The death of Jesus. The resurrection of Jesus.

Will there be other attempts to remove Jesus from history? Absolutely.

For if a man can remove Jesus from the calendar of life, then there is no need to consider His significance. No need to evaluate what His actions really mean. An empty hope winks that there will be no need to kneel before Him.

Philippians 2: 9-10 (NIV):
9 Therefore God exalted Him to the highest place and gave Him the name that is above every name,
10 that at the name of Jesus every knee should bow, in heaven and on earth and under the earth,

If Jesus did not exist, then why did Josephus, Tacticus, Pliny the Younger, and the Sanhedrin write about Him from 93 to 300 A.D. (C.E. for the "No JESUS" crowd)? Were they all deluded to write historical prose for the benefit of their readers?

History records Him.

If Jesus is documented in history, then the next logical step is to look at the claims made about Him and by Him.

One argument attributed to C.S. Lewis is the Liar, Lunatic, or Lord trilemma. We spent some time reviewing this. We broke down each possible choice. Lincoln, Levi, and Legend internalized the possibilities and instilled strength in the plausibility. This argument has been attacked as being flawed, ambiguous, or controversial. Did Jesus claim to be God?

Mark 14:55-64 (NIV):
55 The chief priests and the whole Sanhedrin were looking for evidence against Jesus so that they could put Him to death, but they did not find any.

56 Many testified falsely against Him, but their statements did not agree.

57 Then some stood up and gave this false testimony against Him:

58 "We heard him say, 'I will destroy this temple made with human hands and in three days will build another, not made with hands.'"

59 Yet even then their testimony did not agree.

60 Then the high priest stood up before them and asked Jesus, "Are you not going to answer? What is this testimony that these men are bringing against you?"

61 But Jesus remained silent and gave no answer. Again, the high priest asked him, "Are You the Messiah, the Son of the Blessed One?"

62 "I am," said Jesus. "And you will see the Son of Man sitting at the right hand of the Mighty One and coming on the clouds of heaven."

63 The high priest tore his clothes. "Why do we need any more witnesses?" he asked.

64 "You have heard the blasphemy. What do you think?" They all condemned Him as worthy of death.

High priests were not in the robe tearing business. You don't get this reaction from a claim of being a great teacher. You don't get this reaction from a claim of being a healer. You don't get this reaction from a claim of being a moral man. You get this reaction when someone claims to be God.

Today, we may not understand the significance of Jesus quoting the Old Testament Scripture:

Daniel 7:13-14 (NIV):

13 "In my vision at night I looked, and there before me was

one like a son of man, coming with the clouds of heaven. He approached the Ancient of Days and was led into His presence.

14 He was given authority, glory and sovereign power; all nations and peoples of every language worshiped Him. His dominion is an everlasting dominion that will not pass away, and His kingdom is one that will never be destroyed.

The high priest understood. He got it. And when he got it, he went ballistic. Today, we don't have anger at a claim of a deity because almost daily, you can walk into the inner city and meet someone who claims to be a god. You can watch television and see athletes who think they are gods. You can watch politicians who long for the people to kneel at their feet.

Do a couple of arguments suffice?

So, what would Lincoln, Levi, and Legend say when asked about Jesus' existence?

They have their Scripture, which has been written upon their heart.

They have their calendar, which changed based upon the Life of Jesus.

They have their church, which to this day is still carrying the message of Christ.

They have their testimony of the Love of Christ, which no one can take away.

They have an empty tomb, which stands alone in the history of leaders.

Remember that no man, no death, no life, no angel, no demon, no present, no future, no power, no height, no depth, nor any other thing can take that away from them (Romans 8:38-39 (NIV)).

They have the recorded testimony of the disciples. Liars make very poor martyrs.

They have hope, which is completely lacking in those without Christ.

Is that enough?

If you are wondering, this stone is heavy. Let's lay a stone here.

You decide if Jesus really existed.
You decide what He claimed to be.
You decide how to interpret His claims.
You decide if secular historical documentation impacts your belief.
You decide how to build this foundation.
Everyone may say that Jesus was just a great teacher, when you know more.
See it to the end.

DEFENSE OF FAITH
PART FOUR

Scripture stands. Jesus is documented in history and His claims. What trump card is someone in the world waiting to throw down in the hope that Lincoln, Levi, or Legend would be shaken? Under the anger, arrogance, pride, and resentment lays the largest suit in the frazzled deck of existence: FEAR.

Fourth Question: Why Is There Evil in the World?

When this question is asked, the most obvious thing you should realize is that the person asking the question has no answer. Recently, I saw a video exchange where a lost soul went on to claim that all evil in the world was caused by religion. I smiled, because without Jesus, there would be no difference as to what evil really was.

Next, I emphasized the following point to the boys and had them repeat it several times: If someone's decision about Jesus and salvation hinges upon how you answer a question about evil, then that person is looking in the wrong direction. Freedom comes from knowing your limitations.

My soon-to-be men needed to have thought about the issue, prepared for when the matter arises, and must understand that the ultimate decision was not on their shoulders.

Ezekiel 2:7 (NIV):
7 You must speak my words to them, whether they listen or fail to listen, for they are rebellious.

My sons can answer. They can fail to listen. The game goes on.

Why does an infant suffer from glioblastoma multiforma? Could it be genetics? Possible link to families with neurofibromatosis type I (NFI). Probably not from cell phone use, but there is some squawking about that as a possible cause in adults. Probably not due to work exposure (electromagnetic field vulnerability or occupational hazard - no hard hat). Probably slightly higher in some race categories. Or, could this be the result of a man?

Genesis 3:17-19 (NIV):
17 To Adam he said, "Because you listened to your wife and ate fruit from the tree about which I commanded you, 'You must not eat from it,' "Cursed is the ground because of you; through painful toil you will eat food from it all the days of your life.
18 It will produce thorns and thistles for you, and you will eat the plants of the field.
19 By the sweat of your brow you will eat your food until you return to the ground, since from it you were taken; for dust you are and to dust you will return."

Does not sound like some idyllic utopia. Actually, that kind of sounds like real life.

John 16:33 (NIV):
33 "I have told you these things, so that in Me you may have

peace. In this world you will have trouble. But take heart! I have overcome the world."

So, the boys prepared. They thought about this issue. They looked at the actual words of Jesus telling them that they would have trouble in this life. They took a deep breath and exhaled the responsibility of defending Christ from this attack.

I can't say for sure, but I have a long history of trouble! We met the day I lied to the school bus driver so that I could get off at Gary Cox's house to play kickball. The school instituted a new policy for all bus drivers after that one. Trouble and I met when I fell asleep at the wheel and woke in the hospital with a broken left clavicle and concerned looks from my parents. Trouble and I met with the suicide of my wonderful older brother, Carl. Trouble and I met when my mother stopped her tribulations upon this earth a few weeks ago.

Evil exists. I have seen it in the bullet holes of the folks in the emergency room. I have seen it in the anger and stupor of patients fighting me as I worked to save their lives. I have heard, read, and felt it daily while slogging through the "cursed" ground upon which I have to walk.

Are you ready to teach your progeny about evil? Let's lay a stone here.

While Asking the Fourth Question, we might ponder together: What would people believe if there was no evil?

Nothing bad. No death. No sickness. No suicide. No anger. No fear. No lies.

I would bet that they would not believe in anything. There would be nothing in which to believe. This utopia only exists in

Star Trek, until the Captain needs to take off his shirt and throw down with some enraged alien.

There would be no triumph over evil, as a priori evil did not exist.

But again, evil exists.

But Jesus has overcome the world. Can you be of good cheer (take heart) since Jesus has done this?

You decide how to address evil.
You decide if you want to share your life experience with evil.
You decide the reality of evil existing on this earth.
You decide the source of evil - John 10:10 (NIV) "The thief comes only to steal and kill and destroy; I have come that they may have life, and have it to the full."
You decide the freedom of not having to defend Christ.
Everyone may say that evil in the world disqualifies Christ, but you can rejoice in Jesus overcoming the world.
See it to the end.

DEFENSE OF FAITH PART FIVE

At this point, you can almost see the lost souls throw their hands up in the air and proclaim that they should find pleasure wherever they can as life is meaningless. They should do whatever they want, whenever they want and with whomever they find to go down the rabbit hole with them.

Fifth Question: Why Should I Not Do Whatever I Want in Life?

Please understand, my vision on this issue is clouded by my life experiences.

When Shaun and I cracked open the chest of our cadaver in Gross Anatomy during the first semester of medical school, I was struck by the pitted, black, dirty lungs that were before me. Since I was in medical school, I thought about what disease process had caused all of this damage. While I was thinking about this quietly, our learned professor peered over my shoulder and stated bluntly, "Another smoker."

The impact of that one event has lasted on me to this day, and I offer my patients $100 to stop smoking for 100 days. I take a photo of those patients who claim the prize and I challenge others to follow them down this path. Last week another patient claimed their reward (That makes 18 - $100 bills given to proud quitters!).

While in the Emergency room, the nurse gave me an eye-rolling glance and asked me to see the guy in Bed 4. After a halting medical history was extracted, I finally asked him what was really wrong. His response was, "I've got a problem down there." That vision of erosive ulcers on his genitals from a sexually transmitted disease scarred me for life.

After draining the 9th liter of ascitic fluid from the abdomen of the 40-year-old cirrhotic, who looked 65 years old, I asked him how much alcohol he had imbibed in the course of his life. He glanced to the side and said, "Too much." I put my stitch at the puncture site, since I did not want to be called in the early morning with this patient back in the ER leaking from his paracentesis opening. He was gone within a few weeks.

There are a lot of things in life that are legal to do. There are some that are currently illegal. There are some that used to be illegal but have magnanimously been changed to permissible by the governing bodies. But at what cost?

If you asked my sons the following question, "Does any good thing happen after midnight?"

You will get the same response, "No Sir!"

So, what answer would a 16-year-old man have to the whatever I want in life question?

Lincoln had a great response about the limitations that God placed being actually beneficial to you. He spoke about purity. He spoke about care with drinking.

Ephesians 5:18 (NIV):

8 Do not get drunk on wine, which leads to debauchery. Instead, be filled with the Spirit,

Had Lincoln, Levi, or Legend been challenged in these areas enough to have miles on the odometer to glean practical knowledge at the time of their celebrations? No.

Does this lack of practical knowledge disqualify them from answering?

Not in the least.

I have seen some worldly-wise folks in my life who will definitely tell you their regrets. Why not allow their life experiences to save you some brutal costs. If you cannot learn from others who already know, then how did you learn to speak, learn to read, learn to add, or learn to subtract? We all learn from those who have gone before us. We just get to decide what we want to learn and to whom we want to heed.

They could just say, "Sure, do whatever you want," but that would be dishonest. That response would not be worthy of the responsibility of helping others. That response would not be treating others in a way that you would want to be treated.

If you could save someone the hardship of permanent damage by sharing some wisdom, could you do it? Let's lay a stone here.

My sons know about some of life's opportunities by the words that we have spoken at the dinner table, in the car, and as we walked through life together. My sons have also learned about some of life's opportunities by observing what their parents have actually done, rather than just what they have said.

What has your little one seen and heard from you? The

question of doing whatever you want in life is answered well by living a life worthy of the responsibility of being a parent.

You set the example to be followed by your children. While you are preparing for the ceremony, re-evaluate the example you have been providing. Lay aside the hindrances. Pick up the Scriptures. Brush off the testimony. Raise up the child in the way that they should go (Proverbs 22:6).

> You decide the response to whatever they may want to do.
> You decide where the lines may be drawn.
> You decide how to convey the guardrails of life.
> You decide the costs of crossing the guardrails.
> You decide what example you are providing to your little ones.
> Everyone may say that we should get pleasure wherever we find it, but you know the true costs of missing guard rails.
> See it to the end.

DEFENSE OF FAITH
PART SIX

Life experiences shared by their parents, by others who have gone before them, and by stories gave the boys a starting point. They will have to choose to maintain the expected trajectory or throw off all the limitations and do their own thing. Knowing that the responsibilities of their decisions will be upon their shoulders. The next question is the result of running the argument to the ultimate end:

Sixth Question: If Everyone Around You Rejects Christ, What Are You Going To Do?

Is this even a possibility?

The City of Lake Worth in Florida sent notices to churches that they would have to obtain a business license to continue to have their meetings and operate within the city fiefdom. Churches that have been present for over 100 years would now need a type of city dog tag to be legal. The possibility of Christianity becoming a cultural pariah is not only feasible, but almost guaranteed in the coming societal decline.

The City of Houston, Texas asked some local pastors for the following: "All communication with members of your congregation regarding HERO or the Petition. All speeches, presentations, or sermons related to HERO, the Petition, Mayor Annise Parker, homosexuality, or gender identity prepared by, delivered by, revised by, or approved by you or in your possession." A metropolitan city attacking pastors who may disagree with the current City overlord. As more and more people see these attacks on the church, the sheep will begin to turn from the shepherd.

If you spend a little time flipping through the pages of print, you may find:

The Global War on Christians: Dispatches from the Front Lines of Anti-Christian Persecution, by John L. Allen Jr.

Persecuted: The Global Assault on Christians, by Paul Marshall

Destination Jerusalem: ISIS, Convert or Die, Christian Persecution and Preparing for the Days Ahead, by Chris Mitchell and Mel Cohen

Killing Christians: Living the Faith Where It's Not Safe to Believe, by Tom Doyle

Crucified Again: Exposing Islam's New War on Christians, by Raymond Ibrahim

Christians Burned Alive in Pakistan: Christians Lives Matter, by A. Christian

Arab Spring, Christian Winter: Islam Unleashed on the Church and the World, by Ralph Stice

Persecution: How Liberals are Waging War Against Christianity, by David Limbaugh

And the list keeps growing.

Why?

Because there is so much material.

My Sixth Question to the boys foreshadows what they should expect in their future.

They would be totally unprepared if they had never considered the possibility. If they have considered the likelihood, then they are a step ahead of their peers.

The calendar folks have rejected Christ by changing A.D. (Anno Domini) to C.E. (Common Era). Some cities are attacking Christ and the Church. There will be more cities slinking toward Gomorrah in lock step with Lake Worth, FL or Houston, TX.

Will the boys see others turning away from Christ? Without doubt.

As following Christ becomes more difficult, the plodding line for the exits will grow.

My hope is that they will be in the remnant. They will remain strong. They will be worthy of the Calling of Christ.

An interesting thing happens to those who remain after the crucible has been fired. They are stronger. They are principled. They are pillars.

Could your preparation lead to a young man or women who can stand when everyone else is falling? Let's lay a stone here.

My ability to assess this outcome is limited today. But I have made an attempt to start the process with my sons. We drew the line in the sand. We made a decision. We asked them to address the issue of everyone around them turning from faith in Christ.

Do you feel the need to take the same steps?

Christ will be rejected by this world.

Romans 2:8-9 (NIV):

8 But for those who are self-seeking and who reject the truth and follow evil, there will be wrath and anger.

9 There will be trouble and distress for every human being who does evil: first for the Jew, then for the Gentile;

I Thessalonians 4:7-8 (NIV):

7 For God did not call us to be impure, but to live a holy life.

8 Therefore, anyone who rejects this instruction does not reject a human being but God, the very God who gives you his Holy Spirit.

Interestingly, the prospect of rejecting God was documented years ago. Look around you today and you will see that what was written back then is alive and well today.

You decide how to respond when everyone else turns away.
You decide how to challenge your little one to stand firm.
You decide if your example exhibits this steadfastness.
You decide how quickly this will manifest in your life.
You decide if you want to challenge your little ones to remain strong despite being the only ones left.
Everyone may say the right path is to turn away from Christ, but you know the difference.
See it to the end.

DEFENSE OF FAITH
PART SEVEN

Even if all turned away, we planned for steadfast Men of God who would be able to maintain. We prepared for spiritually based soldiers who would not flee the fight. We established a bar that was high, broad, and clearly communicated.

Does all this preparation wipe away every fear?

Seventh Question: What Are You Afraid Of?

Reality defeats fantasy every time.

This activity was undertaken by almost 16-year-old young men. They were professing that they would stand when all others strayed (noble, but difficult to achieve). They had experienced minimal testing by fire or life (yes, we had tried to protect our children).

Does fear still exist in practice for a 16-year-old young man or woman? Certainly.

Knowing that they could express their fear was one of the freedoms that was purposely arranged for this event. They had an audience, they had an opportunity, and they had their own self-awareness. Would expressing their fears in front of a large group make it easier for them to discuss them with us over the phone or in the safety of our home?

Sometimes, fear is not a bad thing:

Proverbs 1:7 (NIV):
7 The fear of the LORD is the beginning of knowledge, but fools despise wisdom and instruction.

Proverbs 9:10 (NIV):
10 The fear of the LORD is the beginning of wisdom, and knowledge of the Holy One is understanding.

Jesus tells us His perspective about perturbation:

John 14:27 (NIV):
27 Peace I leave with you; My peace I give you. I do not give to you as the world gives. Do not let your hearts be troubled and do not be afraid.

Did the boys have fears? Yes.

They spoke of the coming horizon and the possibility of not doing well in college. This was coming from young men who had not picked a college, not picked a major, not met a beautifully distracting co-ed, and not had to phone home for more money.

Was their response a good assessment of their current state? They had fears.

So, what should we do with these fears? Should they stay in their rooms, close the blinds, keep their heads down, and not venture forward to avoid the increased heart rate, the sweaty palms, or the shallow breath?

My hope is that by facing the simple fact that fear exists in the course of life, they will be stronger. They will know fear when it comes. They will know that they have support. They will know that they can overcome fear.

An unpracticed piano piece is halting, searching, and not very musical.

A practiced piano piece can cause you to close your eyes enjoying the flow of creativity, the tide of emotion, and the spice of expression.

Recognize that fear can be addressed. They can seek wisdom:

Proverbs 11:14 (NIV):

14 For lack of guidance a nation falls, but victory is won through many advisers.

Recognize that they are not alone in fear.

Scripture documents many people being told, "Do not be afraid." Abraham, Hagar, Isaac, Jacob, Israelites, Moses, Joshua, Elijah, Hezekiah's officials, Solomon, King Jehoshaphat, Ahaz, Jeremiah, Ishmael, Johanna, Ezekiel, Daniel, Disciples, Mary and Joseph, Shepherds, Paul and John.

Scripture documents many people telling others not to be afraid. The Lord Jesus and the Angels said this the most, followed by Moses and Isaiah who were next with frequent admonitions. David, Jahaziel, Jeremiah, and Gedaliah said it a few times, while Joshua and Samuel each also gave the instruction. (76 total references in the NIV of "Do not be afraid." With 57 Old Testament and 19 New Testament citations).

Interestingly, some of the same people who were told first to not be afraid, were the same folks telling others not to be afraid later:

Joshua 10:8 (NIV):

8 The LORD said to Joshua, "Do not be afraid of them; I have given them into your hand. Not one of them will be able to withstand you."

Joshua 10:25 (NIV):

25 Joshua said to them, "Do not be afraid; do not be

discouraged. Be strong and courageous. This is what the LORD will do to all the enemies you are going to fight."

From the example above, we must be told not to be afraid. We have to address the battle that is before us which made us fearful. We get to see how the Lord will fight for us. Then, we can tell others not to be afraid. Let's lay a stone here.

My sons stood before a crowd and admitted their fears.
Could your little ones do the same? Could you? I was afraid of messing up the whole process of calling my young men to manhood. The process was undefined. There were no specifics given to me. No foundation upon which to stand. No life experience to extract.
My wife and I would discuss this at night. She would give great suggestions.
My Sunday School lessons would give me food for thought.
The books that I read would give me ideas.
The yearning in my soul would drive me.
You can do it. Just start taking steps. Do not be afraid.

You decide if fear is an enemy to be defeated.
You decide if your fear is keeping you from challenging your child.
You decide why you give fear that power.
You decide what you want in your child related to fear.
You decide why overcoming fear is tantamount to success.
Everyone may say that fear will keep you from achieving your goals, but you know that you can defeat it.
See it to the end.

DEFENSE OF FAITH
PART EIGHT

R epetition helps in life, so I will say to you again, "Do not be afraid!" You can create a ceremony that establishes a time of transition from youth to adulthood for your child. One aspect that I longed to achieve was for the boys to look forward to the event and to state what they were hoping to obtain from their own point of view.

Eighth Question: What Are You Hoping For?

When the veneer of life is pulled back, you see the actual material that has been hidden for aesthetics or shielded from wear and tear. When you ask a young person to tell you their hopes, you peek under the veneer.

There is no right or wrong answer here.

Really, the last 2 questions were clearly communicated with the boys and allowed them room for personal expression. When some of the structure is removed, the genesis of person-hood exposes itself.

Could they state hope right after expressing fear?

Lincoln started by saying that he hoped that when he got to college, he would not be tempted to think that he was too smart for all of this Christianity stuff.

OK, is that his hope, or is it mine? He had the freedom to answer in any way that he saw fit. He verbalized a hope of maintaining his faith. He looked down the road, saw the hurdles and planned to jump high enough to get over the impediments.

Would this one exchange be enough?

Why were we doing any of this in the first place? To have young men who could see themselves as determining the input into the flight plan of their lives.

They can decide. They can plan. They can set goals. All of these things make us an adult. They were beginning to step in the footsteps of adults who had walked before them. With each step, they will stand a little taller (They have all passed me in physical height!). They will lift more authority of adulthood (Mom gave them all their laundry responsibility as a 16-year-old birthday gift). They will be freer (Men unto themselves).

Would I have ever known their hopes without asking?

Take a moment and pull your little one to the side. Stop what you are doing. Stop worrying about tomorrow. Stop thinking about a schedule. Ask them to tell you the things for which they are hoping. You may be surprised. You may find out that you need to adjust your sites in order to assist your future man or woman in reaching the goals they have set for themselves. You may learn something about yourself.

When the young men finished, I turned to the cloud of witnesses present:

"You did not know that you had a part when you came here tonight. But I want to challenge you. You have heard what these young men have said. You have heard their testimony, Scriptures, and answers to some tough questions. You are now their cloud of witnesses. I ask you to pray for these young men. I ask you to remember what they have said. If you are out in the world and see them doing something stupid or going somewhere that they should not be going, you can get up on a chair and give them a good swift kick in the tail!

There was some laughter at that bit of delivery. The reality was that I could not have been more serious. I need help with this process from my friends, family, counselors, and others.

Hebrews 12:1-3 (NIV):
1 Therefore, since we are surrounded by such a great cloud of witnesses, let us throw off everything that hinders and the sin that so easily entangles. And let us run with perseverance the race marked out for us,

2 fixing our eyes on Jesus, the pioneer and perfecter of faith. For the joy set before Him He endured the cross, scorning its shame, and sat down at the right hand of the throne of God.

3 Consider Him who endured such opposition from sinners, so that you will not grow weary and lose heart.

Hope may be forward gazing, but preparation is today.
Have your little one tell you their hopes. Let's lay a stone here.

You decide to take a moment and hear the hopes of your child.
You decide to work to help them achieve those hopes.

You decide to involve others to hear, support, encourage, and challenge your child.

You decide if your hope is to raise strong men and women of God.

You decide if their hopes are important to you.

Everyone may say a child's hopes are not worth thinking about, but you know the value they possess.

See it to the end.

PASSING THE BATON OF FAITH

In the book Rite of Passage: A Father's Blessing, Jim McBride recounted giving his sons a large sword at their ceremony of passage. The idea was unique and challenging. After much consideration, I could not find a sword that I liked, and I could not see my sons keeping up with a large sharp object (You must know your kids!).

So, one day while reading a devotional book, Daily Light for Every Day, Anne Graham Lotz spoke in the foreword about the passing of truth, "…that leads to faith in Jesus Christ from one generation to the next." She used the example of runners in a race passing a baton in order to win the race. This idea resonated with me.

After an Internet search, I found a gentleman who would personalize a baton for me with printing. I chose a golden color with flames on one end. The text would say:

"Lincoln Crea Hoffman. A Man Today."
"Levi Cort Hoffman. A Man Today."
"Legend Cy Hoffman. A Man Today."

After they had answered the eight questions and before they had shared their personal verses and prayed, I informed the audience that we were moving to the next phase of the evening. I introduced my mother, LouEllen Hoffman (Mamou), and my mother-in-law, Carolyn Tipton (Momma-Nut), and asked them to come up to the podium. They were carrying a baton for the boys.

As they were coming to the front of the Grand Ballroom, I quoted Paul:

2 Timothy 1:5 (NIV):
5 I am reminded of your sincere faith, which first lived in your grandmother Lois and in your mother Eunice and, I am persuaded, now lives in you also.

While they were coming up, I recounted the origins of my spiritual life and the role Mamou's dedication had in taking me to church from a young age.

Scripture memory at First Baptist Church Heights in Houston, Texas. Sunday School with a teacher who really impacted my life. Baptism at Houston's First Baptist Church at age 12. True recounting of the origination of the spiritual baton of my life.

Next Mamou and Momma-Nut passed the baton to Rhonda (my beloved) and me.

We thanked them.

Then looking to Lincoln, Levi, and Legend, we said, "This baton represents a spiritual lineage from your grandmothers, to us, and now to you."

Do Not Drop It.

Please understand, I was focused on my sons. I did not see any person's reaction to that declaration. Only in passing have I heard from other attendees how much that portion of the program meant to them.

The boys held the baton and later had them on shelves in their rooms on a small wooden holder.

If you saw the way they were holding the baton at the end of the evening, you would profess that they "got it." They understood. They accepted the weight of the baton. They stepped up to the race with their hand outstretched for their portion of the run.

The baton on the shelf beside their beds symbolizes their participation in the race of life.

Can you impress upon your son or daughter the heady weight of carrying on Jesus Christ to the next generation? It would be much easier to never ask them to step up to the plate. Some would say that the prospect is too much of a load to bear.

Are you going to teach your children by example to keep Jesus unto themselves, or show by example that Jesus should be shared with the next generation and the world?

Luke 19:39-40 (NIV):
39 Some of the Pharisees in the crowd said to Jesus, "Teacher, rebuke your disciples!"
40 "I tell you," He replied, "if they keep quiet, the stones will cry out."

You are guiding the next generation by explicitly showing where your faith originated, what you have done with it, and how you are giving that faith expectation to them. The story is not always about this generation. The actions we take in preparing our little ones may have impacts beyond our understanding. Let's lay a stone here.

If your lineage is missing the stalwarts like Mamou and Momma-Nut, then you can become the "Lois" for possible grandchildren that are not even a glimmer in the eye of their parents.

You decide how to convey your faith to the next generation.
You decide how to show the lineage of faith.
You decide how to challenge your child to carry the faith.
You decide the symbol you will use to show the faith progression.
You decide the meaning of the symbol you choose.
Everyone may say each generation should decide for themselves, but you know that you can raise up your child in the way they should go (Proverbs 22:6).
See it to the end.

A MAN SHARES HIS VERSES

After the passing of the baton, I sat down by my mother (Mamou).

The next portion of the night was Lincoln's, Levi's, or Legend's, and theirs alone.

They were asked to prepare some of their favorite verses and state why they liked the verses or something about the verses that impressed them. They were told that they could use their Bible, in order to relieve any worry about memorization (they had already quoted 40 verses).

Sitting by my mother, I was struck by what Lincoln had prepared, and what each of the other boys had prepared as well:

First Verse
Genesis 1:31 (NIV):
31 God saw all that he had made, and it was very good. And there was evening, and there was morning—the sixth day.

"When the earth has me down and sad, and everything, all I have to do is remember this verse."

A young man needs assurance that God is in control. He can find certainty in the Scripture.

Second Verse

Psalms 90:17 (NIV):

17 May the favor of the Lord our God rest on us; establish the work of our hands for us— yes, establish the work of our hands.

"This verse helps me with the fear of not doing well in college."

Remember, fear is present. Remember the encouragement so often spoken, "Do not be afraid."

Third Verse

Acts 16:31 (NIV):

31 They replied, "Believe in the Lord Jesus, and you will be saved—you and your household."

"This and Romans 10:9-10 are foundational salvation verses and are useful for witnessing to people."

What other hope could I have than a son who can share his faith with others. There is hope!

Fourth Verse

2 Timothy 2:15 (NIV):

15 Do your best to present yourself to God as one approved, a worker who does not need to be ashamed and who correctly handles the word of truth.

"This is the AWANA's verse that explains why Christians need to work and be active in the Church."

Do you mean that all those Sunday nights with the red vests, the jewels of rewards, playing games on the AWANA square were not meaningless? My son was reminded of a verse that he had memorized for AWANA. Thank you, Lord.

Fifth Verse
Revelations 4:8b (NIV):
'Holy, holy, holy is the LORD God Almighty,' Who was, and is, and is to come.'

Although he did not have something specific to say about this, he asked for a moment of patience, and he got out his Greek New Testament and read this verse in Greek. My Latin stinks, and my Greek is worse. Yet, my son together with Midland Classical Academy produced a young man who is able to read biblical Greek in front of 70 guests.

Sixth Verse
Genesis 11:6 (NIV):
6 The LORD said, "If as one people speaking the same language, they have begun to do this, then nothing they plan to do will be impossible for them.

"This is one of my favorite verses, because that is how I like to think, that nothing is impossible for me."

What better way to end this phase of the night than with a wide-open thought?

Nothing is impossible for the coming generation. Let's lay a stone here.

When asked to share their favorite verses, you will be surprised to see what your son or daughter will bring to the table. You will learn from them. You will see God's design in action.

Give them direction. Give them a timeline. Give them freedom. Carefully get out of the way.

You decide to ask your child to hold on to their favorite verses.
You decide to allow them to share the verses without restrictions.
You decide to open your heart and mind to their growth.
You decide to allow others to see them differently.
You decide to say that this is your beloved child in whom you are well pleased.
Everyone may say that sharing your favorite verses before others is hard, but you are asking for a purpose.
See it to the end.

A MAN LEADS A PRAYER

We were winding down to the end of the night, surprisingly on schedule.

While teaching a Sunday School lesson earlier in the year, I realized there was no place in the program where the boys were asked to pray. Sure, in Week Three, they had memorized verses on prayer:

Jeremiah 33:2-3 (NIV):
2 "This is what the LORD says, he who made the earth, the LORD who formed it and established it—the LORD is his name:
3 'Call to me and I will answer you and tell you great and unsearchable things you do not know.'

But they had not actually prayed in the presence of attendees. Yes, they have prayed at the dinner table in our home and at restaurants, but not before a group of witnesses.

So, the night would close with the boys praying before the gathered audience.

I can't honestly tell you the content of their prayers. The pressure of the night was starting to subside, and I may have been a little exhausted from the weeks, months, and years of preparation.

They did pray.

They stood in the Ballroom/Event room with a lapel microphone and led the gathering in prayer.

Once again, I am struck by the fact that at almost 16 years old, these young men were doing something that I probably was unprepared to do at their age. They had poise. They were prepared. They knew what they were going to say.

If glossophobia is the fear of public speaking, and up to 74% of people have that fear (National Institute of Mental Health - 11/23/2013), then seeing and hearing these young men deliver their invocations was exceptional.

By calling upon them to be ready to pray, they had to address their fear.

They had to prepare.

They had to deliver.

The bar is not set too high. They should be ready to do this again. They had accomplished this battle. They can look to others and tell them not to be afraid. They are becoming leaders.

Can you ask this of your child?

Start in their room. Continue at the table. Continue at the restaurants.

Grow to the front of the room with many in attendance.

You can lead on this issue. You can provide an example to follow.

Let's lay a stone here.

A warrior skilled in battle started somewhere. From the first skirmish to the greatest conflict, those in training watched and learned from their mentors.

Try your best not to allow this job to go undone. From the

fountain of prayer springs the living water of faith. There are "… great and unsearchable things that you do not know." Teach your future man or woman to seek out those things on their knees before the Father. Use prayer journals. Use answer logs. Use historical victories. Use your own knees to show them the way.

If you walk away from this book today, have a praying child.

Genesis 25:21 (NIV):
21 Isaac prayed to the LORD on behalf of his wife, because she was childless. The LORD answered his prayer, and his wife Rebekah became pregnant.

2 Samuel 24:25 (NIV):
25 David built an altar to the LORD there and sacrificed burnt offerings and fellowship offerings. Then the LORD answered his prayer in behalf of the land, and the plague on Israel was stopped.

1 Kings 9:3 (NIV):
3 The LORD said to him: "I have heard the prayer and plea you have made before me; I have consecrated this temple, which you have built, by putting my Name there forever. My eyes and My heart will always be there.

2 Chronicles 30:27 (NIV):
27 The priests and the Levites stood to bless the people, and God heard them, for their prayer reached heaven, His holy dwelling place.

Ezra 8:23 (NIV):
23 So we fasted and petitioned our God about this, and He answered our prayer.

A prayerful child will be able to stand when the storms of life come. Have a praying child.

You decide to ask your child to pray.
You decide how to prepare them to be a praying soul.
You decide how to model the praying lifestyle.
You decide if facing Jerusalem like Daniel (Dan. 6:10) is an example you want to follow (Download the application PrayWay: Western Wall Compass (Ethan Glick) - as it will point you in the right direction).
You decide how much you personally value prayer.
Everyone may say that praying should be done in secret, but asking a child to pray before men will help grow their confidence.
See it to the end.

SATURDAY MORNING CAME WITHOUT WARNING

The first order of business on Saturday morning was breakfast with the mentors.

We met at 7:45 am, since the first mentor was to meet with Lincoln at 8:30 am in a quiet room with large chairs, water bottles, and electrical plugs in the middle of the table for any equipment that might be needed.

I arrived early and placed 3 things on each plate in the hotel's restaurant area.

1) A card with the mentor's demographics:

Name, cell phone, address, and E-mail address (with some blank lines for any corrections).

The mentor was supposed to give this card to Lincoln, Levi or Legend as a way to contact them in the future. A card in their Rolodex of life to have as a reference. A name of an adult who was in their corner.

2) A book, Growing in the Gospel, by Brandon Shuman which focused on "…emphasizing the growth of a believer into a disciple."

3) An engraved pen. Due to letter restrictions, the imprint was: MENTORING LCH, MENTORING LEVI, and MENTOR LEGEND.

This allowed me to bless those who had given their time to this endeavor, to provide them with a memento of the event, and to remind them of their call to be a counselor and friend to this young man.

When all had arrived, I briefly introduced each mentor.

I spoke of the significance they had played in both the life of Lincoln and myself. Breakfast was a moment of discovery, because many of the letters sent before this morning had included a schedule referencing all the mentors. They had each been able to see the name and topics of the other mentors prior to arriving at breakfast this Saturday morning.

The gifts were given, the introductions made, and then the challenge was given:

"Today, I am trusting you with one of the most precious possessions of my life. I appreciate all the time and preparation you have undertaken to be here today. I have prayed for you."

As we blessed our food, I called upon the Lord to take the coming few hours and sanctify them. To take the preparation and dedication of these mentors and use them for a life changing encounter with Lincoln, Levi, or Legend. To establish a connection that could be called upon in the future for wisdom, support, guidance, and an open ear.

1 Chronicles 27:32a (NIV):
32 Jonathan, David's uncle, was a counselor, a man of insight and a scribe.

There are those in life who can be called upon to be counselors. There are those who value the prospect of teaching the next generation. There are those that you value as friends. There are family members whose glory is their gray hair.

Proverbs 16:31 (NIV):
31 Gray hair is a crown of splendor; it is attained in the way of righteousness.

Who would you call upon to mentor your child?
Each mentor had a unique role. Each mentor had meaning. Prayers were raised for each mentor. Let's lay a stone here.

You decide who might be a mentor.
You decide how you want to approach them.
You decide what topics you would like them to address.
You decide the order they are going to visit with your child.
You decide how to express your gratitude to them for their time, effort, and commitment.
Everyone may say that you should not bother others with this event, but you know you cannot do everything alone.
See it to the end.

MENTOR ONE

When deciding who would best fill the role of their mentor, I made a list. I thought about folks from my life. I asked the boys who they might want to be a mentor. I considered family members that might rise to the task.

The first person on the list was chosen by Lincoln. He could not come.

Was this a setback? At first, I struggled with the rejection. Doesn't this person not know how important this life changing event will be? What could be more important than helping a young one step over the threshold into adulthood?

If you are wondering, some of my selfishness, pettiness, and immaturity manifested while I prepared for this event.

The first rejection made me reevaluate who I was, reevaluate my motives, and reevaluate who was actually in control of making Lincoln, Levi, and Legend into men. I prayed.

The second on the list actually became Mentor One. Jonathan had known Lincoln for many years as his youth minister at First Baptist Church, Big Spring, TX. Jonathan had led Lincoln in his purity pledge service several years prior during a 'True Love

Waits' program. Lincoln had been to camps under his leadership, had sat in his Sunday teaching, and had enjoyed knowing him as a friend.

Although Jonathan and I had discussed the event previously, the first official phone request came more than 2 months before the event. He agreed, and I was able to place a check in the box by his name. I recorded his title, physical address, phone number and E-mail address. I underlined his name and crossed off one thing on my list. Again, some of the obsessive qualities that drove me were manifesting.

The acceptance started the ball rolling, and after others had accepted, I sent out the following letter:

To the mentors of Lincoln Crea Hoffman:

Scott, (LouEllen and Carolyn), Daron, Jonathan, and Brandon,

First, thank you for your time and commitment to the upcoming event – The Protestant (Christian) Bar Mitzvah (Son of Commandment) - for Lincoln.

Second, I am placing in your capable hands one of the most precious gifts of my life: my firstborn son.

You will have 20-25 minutes to address topics with Lincoln on Saturday morning (March 14th), starting around 8:30 am for the first mentor and starting at 11:00 am for the last mentor. If possible, I would like for all of the mentors to meet with me for breakfast at 7:45 am - understanding that all of you may not be able to make this time.

We will gather again at Noon for a commissioning, laying on of hands with prayer, and the presentation of a ring to a young man. Again, I understand that not everyone may be able to stay this long.

Friday night, March 13th (7:00 pm ~ Historic Hotel Settles ~ Downtown Big Spring, TX) is optional. It will include a piano recital by Lincoln, a time of sharing Scripture, a defense of faith by Lincoln, and the passing of a baton of faith to him.

This is an overview of the planned event. I will be communicating with each of you individually about your topics.

I have prayed for you. I am thankful for you.

Ladd C. Hoffman MD, MBA, MHA
832-971-3611
Lchoffmanmd@sbcglobal.net

After a few weeks of back-and-forth correspondence, the next letter was disseminated to each mentor:

To Jonathan - Mentor One:

As the First Mentor, I would like to share with you a moment.

You have known Lincoln for several years as his Youth Minister. You have already played a role in his life with the purity commitment service. I appreciate you as a father to future godly women, a youth minister, and a friend. You will start his day with his first challenge of adulthood.

Mentor One - Jonathan - Starting with Purity.

Please be guided by your own life, testimony, and experiences. Some biblical verses that crossed my mind are listed below. You may be led to another topic, other verses, or other inputs. This is between you and the Lord. You will have 20-25 minutes to pour your life into the life of the young man standing at the precipice of adulthood.

Thank you for being led by the Holy Spirit.

1 John 2:15-17 (NIV):

15 Do not love the world or anything in the world. If anyone loves the world, love for the Father is not in them.

16 For everything in the world—the lust of the flesh, the lust of the eyes, and the pride of life—comes not from the Father but from the world.

17 The world and its desires pass away, but whoever does the will of God lives forever.

Proverbs 6:23-25 (NIV):

23 For this command is a lamp, this teaching is a light, and correction and instruction are the way to life,

24 keeping you from your neighbor's wife, from the smooth talk of a wayward woman.

25 Do not lust in your heart after her beauty or let her captivate you with her eyes.

Colossians 3:5-6 (NIV):

5 Put to death, therefore, whatever belongs to your earthly nature: sexual immorality, impurity, lust, evil desires and greed, which is idolatry.

6 Because of these, the wrath of God is coming.

1 Thessalonians 4:3-6 (NIV):

3 It is God's will that you should be sanctified: that you should avoid sexual immorality;

4 that each of you should learn to control your own body in a way that is holy and honorable,

5 not in passionate lust like the pagans, who do not know God;

6 and that in this matter no one should wrong or take advantage of a brother or sister. The Lord will punish all those who commit such sins, as we told you and warned you before.

From this letter:

I am available to answer any questions that you may have. Should your preparation require any expense, please allow me to cover those costs, as I have called upon you to fulfill this role. Please be free to challenge Lincoln in any way that you see fit. He can handle the challenge.

I will be providing a card with your name, phone number, address, and E-mail address to Lincoln for him to have a lasting source of wisdom.

The first mentor was chosen. The first topic was chosen.

How do you make your first step?

Do not worry about this question. Start with your list. Start calling. Start getting topics together. The Lord knows your heart. Even if you feel that something is missing, be assured that you are doing your part. So many young souls never get even the slightest attempt made to pour a foundation in their lives for stability.

If I can do this with no prior experience, no prior example, and no certainty, then you can do this.

The ceremony that culminates will be between you and your child and the Lord. That is a great team. Let's lay a stone here.

You decide how to contact the mentors.
You decide what to ask of them.
You decide the best way to convey your desires like addressing purity with your child.

You decide to allow them the freedom to express themselves as led by the Lord.

You decide where your control extends and when you give up the reins.

Everyone may say "there is no one you could trust with this process," but you know that you cannot do it all and your young one may hear someone other than you.

See it to the end.

MENTOR TWO

As I returned to the drawing board, a small amount of confidence had been built with the acceptance of Mentor One. The list was re-examined, and a potential Mentor Two was called.

Great guy. Great father. Great husband. Deacon in the church.

But he had a tennis tournament that weekend, so he and his clan would be out of town. Sorry.

Preparing for your son's or daughter's event will be fraught with hurdles. Will you allow them to knock you down, or simply scrape your knee a little while you continue the race and approach the next impediment?

I got up, brushed off the dirt, adjusted my bandanna, and started running for the next obstacle.

I made a phone call and left a message.

The response came one day later.

Success!!

Mentor Two - Brandon - Applying - the Conversion of Believer to Disciple.

"As the Second Mentor, I would like to share with you a moment. You have known Lincoln for several years as a Tutor and his Editor. I appreciate you as a father, tutor, writer, editor, and Man of God. You have written Growing in the Gospel. My hope is that you can utilize your skill in challenging Lincoln in this very area of your experience and expertise."

Mr. Brandon had already been woven into the fabric of Lincoln's life both in and out of school at Midland Classical Academy. During the previous summer, he collaborated with Lincoln by editing and critiquing the beginning of a novel which was intended to be the first in a series of books written by a budding young author.

Although Brandon was already published on the topic of moving from believer to disciple, I provided some verses for him to think about as well:

Romans 6:22 (NIV):
22 But now that you have been set free from sin and have become slaves of God, the benefit you reap leads to holiness, and the result is eternal life.

John 13:12-17 (NIV):
12 When he had finished washing their feet, he put on his clothes and returned to his place. "Do you understand what I have done for you?" he asked them.
13 "You call me 'Teacher' and 'Lord,' and rightly so, for that is what I am.
14 Now that I, your Lord and Teacher, have washed your feet, you also should wash one another's feet.
15 I have set you an example that you should do as I have done for you.
16 Very truly I tell you, no servant is greater than his master, nor is a messenger greater than the one who sent him.

17 Now that you know these things, you will be blessed if you do them.

1 Peter 2:1-3 (NIV):
1 Therefore, rid yourselves of all malice and all deceit, hypocrisy, envy, and slander of every kind.
2 Like newborn babies, crave pure spiritual milk, so that by it you may grow up in your salvation,
3 now that you have tasted that the Lord is good.

Lamentations 3:25-27 (NIV):
25 The LORD is good to those whose hope is in Him, to the one who seeks Him;
26 it is good to wait quietly for the salvation of the LORD.
27 It is good for a man to bear the yoke while he is young.

Deuteronomy 10:12-13 (NIV):
12 And now, Israel, what does the LORD your God ask of you but to fear the LORD your God, to walk in obedience to him, to love him, to serve the LORD your God with all your heart and with all your soul,
13 and to observe the LORD's commands and decrees that I am giving you today for your own good?

From his letter:
"I am available to answer any questions that you may have.... Lincoln can handle the challenge."

"You are invited to spend the night at the Settles Hotel - I understand that this is difficult as a parent of young souls. Please know that we will have ample coverage to love on your little ones if you bring them. I also would throw out there the possibility of a Date Night / Sleep Over for you and your wife to enjoy one night in Big Spring. Please think about this and confirm your room reservation with me."

The second mentor was chosen. The second topic was chosen.

This was a little easier than the first mentor. Practice does make things easier.

Once you start the process of planning, begin executing your plan, and begin to receive the confirmations, you will see these tasks can be accomplished. Let's lay a stone here.

> You decide how you will handle the rejection of those too busy to be a part.
> You decide how you will get up and keep on going after setbacks.
> You decide if the end will justify the means.
> You decide if progressing from believer to disciple is important.
> You decide other ideas you may want to emphasize.
> Everyone may say this is too big of a project, but you know the end will be fabulous!
> See it to the end.

MENTOR FIVE

Now wait! I used to watch Sesame Street and Count von Count would not agree with the order ONE, TWO, FIVE.

But, if you remember the hurdles, you know that things do not always work out as planned. My mother would often say, "This too shall pass."

I had confidence in the fifth mentor as he and I had discussed this entire matter for years. He knew something had been causing a burr under my saddle. He did not know how to fix me. He only listened patiently as I vented over the years.

When I called him to ask if he would be a mentor, his response was something like this:

"You know, I thought you had given up on the idea, since you hadn't mentioned it in a year or two. I decided not to ask you about it, since you may have changed your mind or something." A true friend even allows me to be quiet about my rants for a while.

So, I perfunctorily asked, "Would you be a mentor for Lincoln?"

"Absolutely."

Mentor Five - Daron - Finishing - Never Quit.

From his letter:
"We crossed paths many years ago at the BSU (Baptist Student Union) in College Station. You are truly one of the few remaining memories of that time in my life. I appreciate you as a father, a friend, a marathoner, and a Man of God. Your life experience has prepared you for this time. I had to put you last, because my heart tells me that no other could follow your presentation."

Some of the verses that I shared with him:

1 Corinthians 9:25-27 (NIV):
25 Everyone who competes in the games goes into strict training. They do it to get a crown that will not last, but we do it to get a crown that will last forever.
26 Therefore I do not run like someone running aimlessly; I do not fight like a boxer beating the air.
27 No, I strike a blow to my body and make it my slave so that after I have preached to others, I myself will not be disqualified for the prize.

1 Chronicles 28:20 (NIV):
20 David also said to Solomon his son, "Be strong and courageous, and do the work. Do not be afraid or discouraged, for the LORD God, my God, is with you. He will not fail you or forsake you until all the work for the service of the temple of the LORD is finished.

Hebrews 12: 1-3 (NIV):
1 Therefore, since we are surrounded by such a great cloud of witnesses, let us throw off everything that hinders and the sin

that so easily entangles. And let us run with perseverance the race marked out for us,

2 fixing our eyes on Jesus, the pioneer and perfecter of faith. For the joy set before him he endured the cross, scorning its shame, and sat down at the right hand of the throne of God.

3 Consider him who endured such opposition from sinners, so that you will not grow weary and lose heart.

You see, I knew Daron.

I knew he would only give his best.

We were riding our bikes together many years ago from Nashville, TN to Natchez, MS on the Natches Trace National Parkway, Daron had put up with me for a solid week. Stinky. Tired. Competitive. But what other idiot would have ridden with him for about 70 miles a day for 7 days on a bike, carrying camping gear? I earned that noble distinction!

Now my physical condition has deteriorated over the years, but Daron has qualified several times, has run before and will be running again in the Boston Marathon. He manifests the physical and mental endurance needed to be a priceless mentor in finishing the race.

So much of the Christian faith is front end loaded. Make a decision. A conversion. A baptism.

So little time is invested in finishing strong. Sadly, a significant percentage of young souls will walk away from their faith in college due to weak foundations, weak expectations, and weak endurance. Some articles delineate the ranges from 60% to 88% (Barna Study 2006, Assembly of God Study, Lifeway Research 2007, Southern Baptist Convention's Family Life Council Study 2002 ~ just references only from Brett Knukle).

My final mentor would address the issue of finishing the race. This takes the idea of the spiritual baton and carries it to a logical conclusion. If you get to the end of the race without the baton, you lose. There are no do-overs. There is no forgiveness of the rules (Hebrews 9:27 Just as people are destined to die once, and after that to face judgment,). You can only complete the race with the baton in hand.

The final topic was easy to choose.

The final mentor was easy to choose.

Some of your choices will be easy. So maybe set some of those selections in the front of the process, since they will build confidence for the battle ahead.

Pick someone who would do anything for you. Give them the task of mentoring. Receive the freedom of having folks who have your back, no matter what. Let's lay a stone here.

The Fifth Mentor was chosen. The fifth topic was obvious and required.

But this did not fill all of the slots.

Doubt began to creep in about how many mentors. Should I change a topic? Am I missing something that needs to be addressed?

Why is that other contact not returning my call?

If you are wondering, you will encounter hard times in this process. These times may be more for your preparation than your child's.

Allow yourself to be challenged, but NEVER QUIT.

You decide who is your finisher.

You decide how important finishing strong is to your child.

You decide how to encourage endurance.

You decide what example you are setting by staying true.

You decide if you need to reassess your own life due to what you are asking of your child.

Everyone may say you can quit, but you know that quitting is not an option.

See it to the end.

MENTOR FOUR

All of you Type A folks are probably mad at me for writing about these mentors out of order, but my selection list had some scribbles and crossed out selections that clearly indicated the difficulties of getting my ducks in a row.

In my heart, I remembered that one of my old Sunday School teachers had really reached me as a young student under his tutelage. Interestingly, he is one of the few teachers that I recall from all the years in classes on Sunday.

So, I had looked him up 2 years before the event on the Internet.

Finding an E-mail address from someone with the correct name was the first step. Sending a message, waiting for a response, and getting a happy response made my day! Thankfully, I had found Tim, and we did reconnect. He sounded excited about the plans and gave me a kind of blessing that I had not anticipated.

When the 2-month window approached before the curtain was lifted, my first call resulted in a voice message for Tim. Two days later another message was left.

Later that night, I got my reply. "No, I've got a speaking engagement that weekend.

Had I failed? Not really. Had I succeeded? Not in filling the fourth position.

Praying, I stopped looking at my plans again, and started listening.

Who has my back? Who do I trust? Who do I know walking the walk of faith and not just talking the talk?

The post-operative surgical rooms of my previous hospital were on the third floor. My office was in the next building over and could be reached via a walkway and down 2 flights of stairs. When I leave the stairwell on the second floor, and turn down the "Staff Only" hallway, I can come to the office of my Doctor friend who patiently listens to me complain about the MEC (Medical Executive Committee), the consult I just received, or some new Core Measure that has me sitting up straight and clapping my hands together like a seal awaiting a rotting fish.

Would he mentor my son?

He has a son of his own. The thought may intrigue him. So, I guess that I will ask Dr. Scott.

Thankfully, he said yes.

Mentor Four - Growing in Faith.

"As the Fourth Mentor, I would like to share with you a moment. You are my friend. I appreciate who you are as a man, a physician, a friend, a runner, and a father. We share some of the same difficulties in our earthly father-son relationships. You have a testimony. I have listened to you speak of faith."

We attend church together. We are in the same Sunday School class. We have been to medical meetings together. We have trained at a shooting event with a Purple Heart Recipient as our instructor. Dr. Scott is also a runner. In his office you will see streams of race medals that he has acquired via sweat equity hanging by his door. He also has photos of his son plastered on his walls.

You may need to look into your life for those who may be traveling the road of parental discovery with you. They have a skill set to call upon. They will probably understand what you are attempting to accomplish and may be challenged to follow your lead.

Some of the verses I shared with him:

1 Samuel 2:26 (NIV):
26 And the boy Samuel continued to grow in stature and in favor with the LORD and with people.

2 Peter 3:17-18 (NIV):
17 Therefore, dear friends, since you have been forewarned, be on your guard so that you may not be carried away by the error of the lawless and fall from your secure position.
18 But grow in the grace and knowledge of our Lord and Savior Jesus Christ. To Him be glory both now and forever! Amen.

2 Thessalonians 1:3 (NIV):
3 We ought always to thank God for you, brothers and sisters, and rightly so, because your faith is growing more and more, and the love all of you have for one another is increasing.

A recent copy of Popular Mechanics magazine had an article entitled "42 Things You Should Know How To Do."
So, let me affirm you with the lessons learned in preparing for the mentors. They will be the ones that God has chosen.

They will have different life experiences to share. They will do a great job.

Dr. Scott sees the world independently from how I see the world. My son needs to have an abundance of counselors (Proverbs 11:14).

Choosing mentors opens the doors of your trust and dependence upon the Lord to guide and direct you. Let's lay a stone here.

The Fourth Mentor was chosen. The fourth topic was chosen.

Yes, I know, I missed the Third Mentor. One. Two. Five. Four. Not the best at keeping order.

There was definitely a reason. Again, a time for prayer arose.

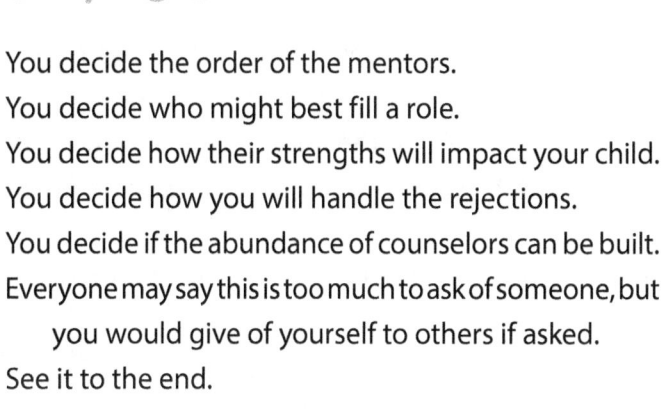

You decide the order of the mentors.
You decide who might best fill a role.
You decide how their strengths will impact your child.
You decide how you will handle the rejections.
You decide if the abundance of counselors can be built.
Everyone may say this is too much to ask of someone, but you would give of yourself to others if asked.
See it to the end.

MENTOR THREE

Out of order, but surprisingly falling in place with each day. My final choice of mentor turned into a team approach. What better way to pass on spiritual faith than tapping the matriarchs of the family and allowing them to look their grandchild in the eye and speak from their heart. I could share with you another rejection story, but let me affirm that there were others offered the gift of mentoring. There were others that I thought were certainly the ones to share. But I was wrong.

Let me tell you a little about the next team of mentors.

My Father-In-Law had been called P-nut most of his life. When he was young, he went around selling sacks of peanuts. As he got into school, the name stuck. When he ran his wrecker service and his service station, his shirts had "P-nut" stitched above the left pocket. It followed quite well that when the first grandkid arrived, he was called Poppy Nut.

If you are married to P-nut and have grandchildren, you might get stuck with the following loving name: "Momma-Nut."

No, she is not bothered in the least by the name.

Actually, she is known far and wide by Momma-Nut, and she

fits the bill quite well. My Mother-In-Law accepted the offer of being one of the mentors for Lincoln.

When a little grandchild looks at you, you will pretty much take whatever name that the little crumb cruncher can pronounce. My mother kind of wanted "Momma-Lou." But a developing tongue and a 2-syllable preference over a 3-syllable name led to "Mamou." So, when she was asked to be a mentor, I had little doubt that she would graciously accept. Now this is cheating a little since she would do almost anything for me that I would ask of her. Thank you, Mom, for being Mom, you were a great Mamou.

Mentor Three (Really a Team) - Carolyn (Momma-Nut) and LouEllen (Mamou) - Loving - Lineage and Future.

From their letter:
"Mamou - You are my rock. I trace my spiritual lineage to you. I appreciate you as a mother, a teacher, a Proverbs 31 woman, and a tremendous grandmother. Without a doubt, you have a testimony of overcoming. I hope you have the freedom in Spirit to pass on your wisdom."

"Momma-Nut - Thank you for allowing me to be your Son-In-Law. I appreciate you as a mother, a servant, an example to my kids, and a special grandmother. You will bring laughter to all you encounter. I am thankful that you invest in my children."

Some of the verses I shared with them:

Ephesians 6:1-4 (NIV):
1 Children, obey your parents in the Lord, for this is right.
2 "Honor your father and mother"—which is the first commandment with a promise—

3 "so that it may go well with you and that you may enjoy long life on the earth."

4 Fathers, do not exasperate your children; instead, bring them up in the training and instruction of the Lord.

1 John 3:1-2 (NIV):

1 See what great love the Father has lavished on us, that we should be called children of God! And that is what we are! The reason the world does not know us is that it did not know Him.

2 Dear friends, now we are children of God, and what we will be has not yet been made known. But we know that when Christ appears, we shall be like Him, for we shall see Him as He is.

Galatians 6:9-10 (NIV):

9 Let us not become weary in doing good, for at the proper time we will reap a harvest if we do not give up.

10 Therefore, as we have opportunity, let us do good to all people, especially to those who belong to the family of believers.

Proverbs 17:6 (NIV):

6 Children's children are a crown to the aged, and parents are the pride of their children.

3 John 1:3-4 (NIV):

3 It gave me great joy when some believers came and testified about your faithfulness to the truth, telling how you continue to walk in it.

4 I have no greater joy than to hear that my children are walking in the truth.

The Third Mentors were chosen. The third topic was chosen.

You might think that I had a large sigh of relief at this point with all the slots filled. Not really. I couldn't get in the way of what the Lord had planned. I had to trust each adviser to prepare. I had to walk away and not try to control something else that was beyond my pay grade. I would send encouraging letters or E-mails, but I never bothered them again about their topics.

Are 3 mentors enough? Are 4 mentors enough?

Again, there is no exact answer to this question. You can find your point of contentment. You can decide. You may even reject the concept of mentors entirely. For me, Lincoln, Levi, and Legend needed to hear from others besides me. They needed different perspectives.

Does your little one need other inputs? Let's lay a stone here.

Each Mentor received a schedule for Saturday morning. Each received a topic.

08:30-08:55 - First Mentor - Jonathan - Starting with Purity.

09:00-09:25 - Second Mentor - Brandon - Applying - Converting Believer to Disciple.

09:30-09:55 - Third Mentors - Momma-Nut and Mamou - Loving - Lineage and Future.

10:00-10:25 - Fourth Mentor - Scott - Growing in Faith.

10:30-11:00 - Fifth Mentor - Daron - Finishing - Never Quit.

11:30 - Commissioning Time - Laying on of Hands, Prayers, and Presentation of Ring of Adulthood

You decide on mentors.

You decide on topics.

You decide the timing.

You decide the training.

You decide the completion.

Everyone may say this is too hard, but you know the difficulty is in not trying to love your child with everything.

See it to the end.

THE MENTORS HAVE SPOKEN, LET'S FINISH STRONG

As you have probably noted, I'm a little obsessive compulsive in my life. I had a remote switch with a button that I could turn on a lamp in the conference room to notify the mentors that they had 5 more minutes to finish their time with the boys.

We finished the mentor meetings on time. The boys had a moment to take a break, then we all gathered in a room for the next portion of the ceremony.

We had the young man sit in a comfortable chair at the end of the room and all the family and friends who remained circled the room. We had each person lay hands on the boys and pray over them. Some did not pray; some just placed their hands on them. Others wept as they prayed. Lastly, Rhonda and I placed our hands on them and prayed. It was a prayer of challenge, commissioning, and thankfulness for this moment in their lives.

Many have spoken to me about the impact that this time of prayer had on their experience of the Bar Mitzvah. When I was commissioned as a deacon at church, a similar event marked a threshold in my life. The boys would have this reference point in their lives forever.

If you want to take a deep breath and rest for a minute, you are not alone. The pressure of the preparation, the planning, and the performance is a little much. What could possibly add to an already impactful event?

When I was training to be a surgeon, I had a ring that my grandfather had given me. It was silver with an oval turquoise stone. Mac Mac had purchased the ring from a street vendor in Santa Fe, New Mexico. It was a symbol of him, a memory of him, and a precious possession.

Since I must wash my hands often in preparation for surgery, I lost the ring during my training. Not only was I sad, but I was also kind of defeated and mad at myself. I walked around the parking lot where I remembered parking the day before. I asked around the operating room preparation area. I asked the scrub technicians. No luck.

As a gracious surprise years later, my wife had taken an old college ring of mine and our original wedding band and visited a master jeweler in Big Spring, TX. Jay Phinney at The Karat Patch allowed the boys to watch him as he melted the gold and fashioned a ring with turquoise that mirrored my grandfather's ring. There was even a portion of gold left over after the event. Rhonda and the boys surprised me one night at dinner with the gift of the ring. I wear it every day.

With the portion of the left-over gold, Rhonda and I returned to Jay and asked him to fashion a ring like mine with the birth stone of each boy instead of the turquoise. As Lincoln was first, this portion of the ceremony was unknown to him. His ring had a symbol on the side indicating that he was firstborn: a "T" with a dot above the top bar, much like when I write on a prescription to take one pill with a specific frequency. Often, I will refer to him as "Number 1."

Each boy's ring was specific to them – specific to their birth stone – specific to their birth order – containing gold from my college ring and our wedding ring. Lincoln had one dot, one bar and an aquamarine stone. Levi had two dots, two bars, and a sapphire stone. Legend had three dots, three bars, and a peridot stone.

While standing on the beach in Belize years ago, I married a young couple and provided some biblical insight into the symbolism of a ring. Since the boys were at a monumental moment in their lives, I provided some of that insight again:

Genesis 41:41-43 (NIV):

41 So Pharaoh said to Joseph, "I hereby put you in charge of the whole land of Egypt."

42 Then Pharaoh took his signet ring from his finger and put it on Joseph's finger. He dressed him in robes of fine linen and put a gold chain around his neck.

43 He had him ride in a chariot as his second-in-command, and people shouted before him, "Make way!" Thus, he put him in charge of the whole land of Egypt.

A ring can symbolize the authority to lead a nation. It can grant power, privilege, and prestige. It can change how the world perceives the person wearing the ring. We wanted these rings to represent the new station in life of each young man.

Luke 15:21-22 (NIV):

21 "The son said to him, 'Father, I have sinned against heaven and against you. I am no longer worthy to be called your son.'

22 "But the father said to his servants, 'Quick! Bring the best robe and put it on him. Put a ring on his finger and sandals on his feet.

A ring can symbolize forgiveness and restoration from a life of sin. It can restore fellowship and position in a family. It can change how the wearer sees himself or herself. We wanted these rings to tell of our forever love and forgiveness to these young men prior to them venturing into the world.

Finishing with a ring and a declaration of manhood.

There will never be a day that this ceremony can be undone. The meaning of the ring will never fade. You can come up with your own way to mark the transition. If a ring can symbolize leading a nation and forgiveness from sin, then it can symbolize attaining adulthood.

You decide.

UNINTENDED SIDE EFFECT

Mrs. Sherry came to us and said that these two young men were "our kids." The two Turkish basketball players were on the local Junior College Team at Howard College. Tolonya did not like us and did not hang around, but Koray came into our home and became our fourth son.

You see, the dorms at the college were closed at Thanksgiving and Christmas and these young men could not go all the way to Türkiye in a short time. As a result, our church established a ministry to open our homes to them and share Jesus by serving as a family away from home.

If you ever want to really experience fear, smile as a 6' 8" basketball player stands in front of your refrigerator and looks for something to eat. We had told Koray to make himself at home and that our food was his food. I did not know that TWO (2) foot-long sandwiches (from Subway®) could be wolfed down in one sitting, but I quickly learned!

Koray watched as I worked with my sons, played with my sons, challenged my sons, and taught my sons. Interestingly, although English was difficult for him at first, he began to see us as not only as hosts, but loving parents. He joined us with his heart, and Rhonda and I grew to love him as one of our own.

When his time at Howard College ended, we helped him find another team in Arkansas. After a semester, he decided to stop playing and return to Türkiye. I had a meeting with him on the mid-court logo and told him that quitting can become a habit. He listened to that exchange and it changed his life's course. He applied for a student visa and was granted one (which is a miracle), and with all of the colleges in the United States, he chose Midland College in the city where we lived. He graduates in May with an RN degree, since we had talked about the fastest way to a green card would be choosing an underserved profession. His dedication is amazing.

God knows what my goals are for the young men in my life.
He knows that so well, that He has chosen to place other young men under our wings to be challenged and to learn.
If you decide to go down this road, I ask you to be ready to be used by the Lord in the lives of kids that you have not even met, because God has the plan to use you as a tool to minister and love on them as a father and mother of honor.

Evan plays the drums at our church, and attends East Texas Baptist University in Marshall, TX. On his first Sunday, Rhonda said we need to take him to the gas station, fill up his car, and feed him, as we know how tight things can be for college kids. He looked at us with an inquisitive eye at our first meeting, but he decided getting some gas and food was worth his time. Every Sunday and most Wednesday nights after choir practice, we take Evan and love on him, feed him, and fill up his car. He lived with us last summer to decrease the travel burdens for his Church job and to survive closed dorms, and he is scheduled to be at our home this summer. Evan became my fifth son.

I'm not sure how to do all of this father stuff, but I am sure that God has blessed me with a full quiver and I need to be able to equip these young men in a tough world.

You will never know the direction that this planning and preparation will lead. Rhonda and I have been blessed with the chance to minister, love, encourage, challenge, and lift up these young men. Please choose to be available to do the same in the manner you see fit.

You can never guess what the Lord has planned.

FIRST BORN LINCOLN CREA HOFFMAN

In an effort to allow you to see this event from several sets of eyes, I have included responses from the young men who participated, from some mentors, and from some guests who attended. I sent a set of questions to each group. The responses that follow are from the participants in the front of the ballroom, from the library where the mentor meetings occurred, and from the audience experiencing the event.

Lincoln is my firstborn. He is my absent-minded professor whose brain is in another universe. I have begged and pleaded with him to get a haircut. I spent the most time with him, as I was not in medical school when he was born:

At the time of this writing, my Bar Mitzvah was eight years ago.

1) I am thankful for the process of a Protestant Bar Mitzvah because:

Through this ceremony, I was given the gift of knowing exactly when I became a man. From the moment I turned 16, I have had a constant reminder on my hand (my manhood ring) that calls me to a higher purpose. The importance of this knowledge and calling cannot be overstated in my opinion. I am thankful that I have been able to carry with me the confidence of manhood and a reminder of its importance daily since my Bar Mitzvah.

2) The best part of the process was:

The best part of the process was the encouragement and community my family and friends provided on the night of the event. The preparation that went into the event sometimes felt monotonous, especially to my 16-year-old self. On the night of my Bar Mitzvah, the fact that a whole room was present to witness my commissioning for manhood immediately drove home the importance of the moment in a spiritual sense. A close second would be when I was prayed over by my friends and family immediately before receiving the ring.

3) The hardest part of the process was:

For me as a 16-year-old, the preparation was the hardest part. Reading dense theology, studying apologetics, and memorizing verses were difficult and required a lot of prodding from both parents. (Today, I am thankful for this prodding!)

4) The baton that was passed to me means:

That I am the inheritor of my family's faith, honor, and history, and it is my responsibility to guard each of these virtues and have the ability to pass them on to my friends, acquaintances, and future family.

5) The ring on my finger means:

That the responsibility for my life decisions rests upon my shoulders and mine alone. That if I found myself in a strange city with $20 and no plan, that I would need to grab my bootstraps and step into what the Lord has for me there. That I will lead a family one day (God willing).

6) If you are a parent and asking me if you should do this with your children, then I would say:

You absolutely should follow in my dad's footsteps in replicating a Christian Bar Mitzvah. I (as someone who's been the subject of one) will be continuing this tradition for my children one day. I strongly believe than people who are not told when to become adults may easily never become one. I see my peers, classmates, and coworkers living their lives in continual adolescence. Commissioning your children to manhood and womanhood is a wonderful blessing that you can give them.

7) If you are a kid whose parents are planning this for you, I would tell you:

Take the opportunity to think deeply about what kind of man or woman you want to be one day! If you can answer this question within yourself, you'll have a target to aim for. Seek some wisdom from wise counsel about your target, and prayerfully consider the importance of the fact that you've been given the opportunity to inherit adulthood. Growing up is simultaneously fun and terrifying, but God is with you wherever you go.

8) If I could change something about the process, I would change:

I personally appreciated the entire process. I wouldn't change anything about the process that I had. But for you, the reader, make sure that the process for your kid/relative/self is tailored to be the best for the person who is becoming a man/woman. It should be just as much for them as an individual as it is for the family and friends.

9) My hope for you is:

That you will be encouraged to follow in my family's footsteps and implement this commissioning to adulthood into your children's lives.

10) My final thought:

As I grow older, I am thankful that my mom and dad took the initiative to put together the Protestant Bar Mitzvah for myself and my brothers. I believe that we have been made much better men for it and that it has started a tradition in our family that will go on for a long time.

SECOND BORN LEVI
CORT HOFFMAN

L evi is my happy child. He has a smile that will fill a room, a heart that is soft and loving, and a strength that was acquired by hours in the weight room. His responses were handwritten on a piece of paper, and I will do my best to get the responses conveyed to you.

1) I am thankful for the Protestant Bar Mitzvah because:

The process of my Bar Mitzvah was not only impactful to me, but also impactful to others. My story of the event is unique. Many people have asked me what my ring means, and that simple question has presented a plethora of ministry opportunities. I have shared the gospel with many curious onlookers, who were curious about the meaning of my unique looking ring. Additionally, I am thankful for the immense amount of time I was able to spend with my dad. It gives a young boy confidence in the world when his father has declared him a man, prays for him, and desires the best for him. I believe that as time passes, our Western society keeps driving the age at which a boy is considered a man up and up. For the majority of human history, a boy became a man at around 13 years old. I believe that a younger transition to manhood is not beneficial for a young boy.

2) The best part of the process was:

I think the best part of the process was hard to choose. I loved the symbolism used in the ceremony. The ring, baton, defense of faith. I think the best part had to be the mentors that I had. That was so critical, and I am glad to have all the men and women mentoring me today.

3) The hardest part of the process was:

The hardest part was definitely the Scripture memorization. The amount that Dad had us digest felt like a lot! Luckily, Dad made sure we were prepared.

4) The baton that was passed to me means:

The baton meant to me that the authority my father holds was being passed down to me in a way. I know the biblical symbolism of the ring, but it felt like the baton represented authority more.

5) The ring on my finger means:

I felt the ring represents a daily reminder of manhood and trust. I received the ring and it symbolizes my transition to manhood. I felt it also represents trust between my father and me.

6) If you are a parent and wondering whether you should do this with your children, then I would say:

I would absolutely recommend this ceremony to you and your children. Ascension to manhood is integral to a man's development. If the process is done in a way that is similar to this, it will provide your child with clarity. Clarity with how you view them as well as how they view themselves.

7) If you are a kid whose parents are planning this for you, I would tell you:

Get ready! Prepare! Take it seriously. This is a serious event filled with symbolism and love. Do not take it for granted.

8) If I could change something about the process, I would change:

I think ordering the mentors differently would be beneficial. Maybe have the mentors meet with the man at different times. Like one mentor meets with him a few weeks before the ceremony over a cup of coffee. Spread them out a little. Cramming all the mentors into one morning shortens the mentor's desired time and overwhelms the young man.

9) My hope for you is:

Take this seriously! And parents, after you declare your son a man, treat him like it. There are no takebacks to this. If you say he is a man, let him be a man. You can interpret that however it applies to your family.

10) My final thought:

Do it right, because your son or daughter will not be 16 more than once! Guide the kiddo through it and love on them. This ceremony does not need to be as lavish as mine - the symbolism and heart behind it are what counts!

THIRD BORN LEGEND
CY HOFFMAN

Legend grew up with big brothers and hung around their friends. He left high school at 16 years old, started college and went to Cañon City, Colorado at 17 for a year at Worldview at the Abbey. He is my bull in the China shop!

1) I am thankful for the Protestant Bar Mitzvah because:

It showed that my parents valued me enough to put the responsibility of manhood on me, their child. I have this idea that when you are younger, obedience comes out of fear, fear of getting spanked or punished. But as you transition through adolescence, you obey out of respect for your parents, because of the things they have done for you and how they live. The Protestant Bar Mitzvah was an integral part of that transition from fear to respect. This idea is biblical, Colossians 3:20-21 tells us, "Children obey your parents in everything, for this pleases the Lord." This is the fear aspect that I spoke of, obeying in everything. The respect aspect comes later, "The eye that mocks a father and scorns to obey a mother will be picked out by the ravens of the valley and eaten by the vultures (Proverbs 30:17)." The fear to respect transition calcified for me in the ring ceremony that occurred, and I am thankful for that.

2) The best part of the process was:
I personally really enjoyed performing the speech of memorizing the Scriptures and facts. I enjoy public speaking and that part of the process was a blast, controlling the room, being the only one who knows the information, and getting the opportunity to play the violin for the people I love.

3) The hardest part of the process was:
The hardest part of the process was memorizing and understanding all the evidence that was needed. Reading a large book and memorizing Scripture after Scripture was assuredly the most difficult but rewarding part of the experience.

4) The baton that was passed to me means:
The baton is a passing of legacy, a family crest in my mind. The name "Hoffman." The honor you must hold is given to you through the baton.

5) The ring on my finger means:
I just finished reading Beowulf for my college class. In this story, a mighty warrior fights a demon, but an interesting thing I learned in this story is that older lords and kings would sometimes be called a "ring-giver." In ancient times, kings would reward warriors and men for their courageous service and actions with gold rings or armbands. The rings were a sign of appreciation that the men took on the responsibility and excelled at serving. Likewise, my ring means that I must take responsibility for my actions. It is a daily reminder that I serve others not only as a Christian but as a man with thoughts and deeds for which I will be held accountable. The ring on my finger is my favorite

part of the process; it separates me from the crowd. It helps me be in the world, but not of it. Few 16-year-olds have a ring on their finger and act like a man.

6) If you are a parent and asking me if you should do this with your children, I would say:

To tell your kids, "You are a man or woman." However, you still have them living in your home and your inner desire to traditionally parent them is challenging. After you say this, you have to follow your word. If your child wants to do something, you express your opinion and the consequences, but you cannot force them to do what you want. This manifested in my life when my mother allowed me to do certain things, because I was given the authority to make decisions. It is a hard thing to "let go of" in this sense, but it is absolutely necessary if you do a Protestant Bar Mitzvah. If you keep your iron grip on your children, it would be perceived as if the ceremony did not mean anything, as if you were not serious when you declared your child a man. This decision comes with ramifications, and I would be wary of these yet I would not trade this experience or what it means to me for anything. I am saying that it is absolutely worth the difficulty of trusting your child to make the right decision, for the benefit of being able to make the decision at all. It reminds me of God giving Adam and Eve free will, which their choice to obey Him actually mattered.

7) If you are a kid whose parents are planning this for you, I would tell you:

Your parents might be scared that if you have the freedom to do whatever you want, that you might start living a worldly life. I just want to tell you that is not what happened to me. This Bar Mitzvah puts the parents in a loving, supporting and advisory role. What I mean, is that I now respect their opinion so much more and seek it out. Because of this ceremony, the rules for engagement are clearly defined. Whenever an issue arises, I can contact my mentors or parents, but I have the final say in what to do. It has never benefited me to go against what my parents say when I ask for their advice. It is so nice to have all this wisdom available after this process.

8) If I could change something about the process, I would change:

I would have changed the number of times we rehearsed the whole thing. We only did one full practice run standing in the room with the chairs and everything, but I now believe that I would have been a much better speaker had we done the practice 2-4 times instead of just once with the stage set up. That would take some pressure off and help me edit the harder to communicate parts of the speech.

9) My hope for you is:

You should seriously consider having a Protestant Bar Mitzvah, or a similar discussion with your children. I want to emphasize that this is not the only way to do it. What is crucial to understand is the principle or idea behind it. The idea of loving your kids enough to let go, and tell them you are letting go by declaring them a man or woman.

10) My final thought:

The transition from fear of parents to respect is the most important part to grasp, and my final thoughts revolve around this. Expressing how valuable my Bar Mitzvah was to my transition to manhood is difficult. Without this, I would not be as confident in who I am as a person, I would struggle with my understanding of manhood, and I would not trust my parents in the way I do now.

It helps to have wise people to seek counsel when a big decision in your life comes up. Stay in contact with your mentors, it is one of the most important parts of the process and part of what makes it so special. I am so grateful my parents had a Protestant Bar Mitzvah for me.

MENTOR LOUELLEN HOFFMAN

My beloved mother, Lou Ellen Hoffman (3/17/1943 - 1/24/2023), was moving some leaves after a storm passed through Houston on January 24, 2023. She felt bad, called EMS, got her driver's license, got some of her medication bottles, locked the house and was outside when the ambulance arrived. They did CPR for 45 minutes and never restored a pulse. Here are her responses to my questions for the mentors:

1) Being a Mentor for these young men means:

I am honored to be included in the ones chosen to mentor these fine young men. It is both an honor and a responsibility that I pray I will be worthy to participate.

2) The best part of the process was:

The most moving part of the ceremony was our praying over them individually while putting our hands on their shoulders. Prayer is the best thing we can do for them.

3) The hardest part of the process was:
Choosing the most appropriate Scriptures to share with the three young men. So many Scriptures are so good, but being led to the right one for the right boy was indeed soul-searching.

4) My preparation included:
Choosing Scripture.
Praying about what to share.
Making sure I didn't say too much.

5) If I could change anything about the process, I would change:
I thought the time allotted to the mentors was a little long. I was concerned that the young man would be overwhelmed after a while.

6) My final thoughts:
I hope the young men realize how much they are loved and appreciated and hope they appreciate the time, preparation and effort that was bestowed upon them. Especially, I hope that they will remember the Scriptures they memorized and be able to share with others their knowledge of Jesus and His Word.

MENTOR CAROLYN T. TIPTON

My Mother-In-Law is Carolyn T. Tipton, also known as Momma-Nut, is a joy and a source of laughter in our family. We have traveled the world together, and she lived with us for one and a half years while Rhonda went through breast cancer. I am blessed that she allowed me to be her Son-In-Law. Her responses:

1) Being a Mentor for these young men means:

Being a mentor to me is just a different name for Grandmother. When you become a grandparent, it is a special time of your life. You have more time without so many pressures of life beating upon you at the same time. Being a mentor just puts words to what is normal for a grandparent. I got to watch them grow from being a beautiful baby to handsome responsible young men.

2) The best part of the process was:

The best part of the process was actually seeing them defend their faith. They each were so well prepared with Scripture as well as playing the piano or violin. The fact that they were so comfortable sharing their faith in front of an audience with such confidence lets me know that this will be a part of their life forever. Undoubtedly, sharing their faith will continue for the rest of their lives.

3) The hardest part of the process was:

The hardest part of the process was watching and listening to them get ready. How often they had excuses for not practicing piano or violin cannot be counted much less studying the Bible. But they all 3 pulled through. Oh, how I prayed for them to focus and learn.

4) My preparation included:

My preparation started with them from birth. They were constantly in my prayers to be obedient children, to learn all they could, to get along with others, and to love God and accept Him as their Lord and Savior. I have also been praying for them as they study in college, and then find a God-fearing wife to share life with.

5) If I could change anything about the process, I would change:

I cannot think of anything I would change about the Protestant Bar Mitzvah. These are the only ones I know about, but when I traveled to Israel, we saw the celebration happening in the streets. There was loud music and dancing. Then at the prayer wall, there were women standing on ladders looking over at the men as they celebrated. I do not know if these young men were taught anything about the Bible.

6) My final thoughts:

My final thoughts are how blessed I am to have such wonderful children and grandchildren. I am so thankful to have been able to watch them grow up and become the Godly men they are today. I am looking forward to what God has in store for them and also looking forward to becoming a great grandmother someday. My daily prayers are for them to seek God's guidance daily.

Hope this is what you wanted. So proud of you and the boys. Maybe more people will consider the importance of Christian training at an early age.

Love you,
Momma-Nut

MENTOR DARON MOORE

Daron and I attended college together. He and I rode the Natchez Trace together over 7 days and still maintained a friendship! He is my sounding board. He is my encourager. His life experience is valuable to me and others in his life. He is a CASA (Court Appointed Special Advocates) volunteer and represents his client with passion and diligence. His responses to my questions for mentors:

Mentor Thoughts

My name is Daron Moore and I was one of the mentors for both Lincoln and Levi. I also served as a Master of Ceremony of sorts at Legend's Protestant Bar Mitzvah, but have no role with him post ceremony.

As background, I have been a father to four young women who are each older than Ladd's oldest boy. Having four teenage girls in the same house at the same time is challenging. But my experience does not extend directly to young men, so being a mentor while recognizing a knowledge and experience gap can be more challenging. Regarding Ladd, I have known him since college and we have stayed in close contact ever since. I was in Ladd and Rhonda's wedding party and Ladd was in mine as well. One highlight of our friendship was a week-long bicycle trip on the Natchez Trace Parkway in 1993. If you fail to know someone after something like that you never will. We have watched each other over the years, commiserated at times, and celebrated together when possible. I did not accept the mentor role without the knowledge of Ladd's values and what he was trying to accomplish with his sons.

When Ladd initially started talking about a Protestant Bar Mitzvah, I thought the idea was interesting and unique. Since the process is ongoing in the mentoring phase, the jury is still out, but overall, I support the concept and am glad to be participating. Positives include staying in the lives of the young men and hearing about their dreams, foibles, thoughts on Ladd and family issues, and future plans. I cannot say I have offered as much value as I had hoped. The primary negative includes not being plugged into the young men's lives as much as I would like since the ceremonies took place, but I will accept the fault for this, of course.

The use of a point in time ceremony to signal the move of a boy to a man is unusual in American culture. When I describe this event and subsequent expectations to others the response is typically supportive, but surprising. The ceremony's use of Scripture preparation and the ceremonial passing of the ring and baton were well done in all three instances, and the young men are to be commended for their diligence in preparation. The expectations were clear.

After the ceremonies the young men were still 16 years old, however, and at times, of course, behaved like it. Expectations should not include an immediate maturation beyond their years. The expectation bar, however, was clearly set and there is much value in this.

My preparation for the ceremony for Lincoln and Levi was to prepare a 30-minute private discussion with each with the theme, assigned by Ladd, being "Finishing Strong." I enjoyed watching the boys react to 20-50 year thinking and how values will impact their lives. I hope they remember something of that talk; I know we discuss pieces of it at times still. The most surprising aspect for me has been how much my thinking has changed as I have matured and changed since the ceremonies. None of us are static, and I have tried to impart that further lesson since the ceremony itself. There is a need for transparency between mentee and mentor, certainly.

My greatest disappointment in the process to date is the inability to stay as involved in the young men's lives as I would have liked and expected at the time of the role acceptance. This could change at any time, of course, and I am open and welcoming to that if need be. I was able to provide guidance to Lincoln when he faced an issue early in his college career and I believe our relationship cemented by the mentor role offered real value to Lincoln. I hope both Lincoln and Levi will be willing to seek guidance on any number of topics in the future. Undoubtedly, I will not be able to help in every instance, but I believe that their understanding that incomplete knowledge can lead to acceptable solutions is a key aspect of growth. Furthermore, elders with different experiences can offer valuable insights to find a solution.

There has been another area in which I have comments. As background, in addition to supporting Ladd and his boys, I have worked for years as a volunteer in a local elementary school with at-risk children one-on-one an hour a week. I have also served as a court appointed special advocate (CASA) volunteer with a young man for over a year. The differences between the three cases - at-risk elementary school kids, CASA boy, and Ladd's boys - could not be more distinct.

In summary, I believe that I add significant value to the CASA boy as he is preparing for young adulthood. I represent him as a Surrogate Parent in his education and stand for his best interests in housing and life experiences. Putting together a team of educators, residence staff, adoption staff, state employees, and the court system for the betterment of one individual is gratifying and an honor. Due mainly to the positive home situation provided by Ladd and Rhonda the mentored young men do not require extensive involvement. Let me be clear that this is no one's fault unless it is mine, however. It is simply the way of the world in some instances; some have more offered to them than others.

Therefore, I have concluded that what Ladd has done is to be greatly commended. Setting expectations with an infrastructure in place for future success is a wonderful building block for any young man. I am hopeful and optimistic that Ladd's boys will continue to develop into the men they appear to be on track to become. However, they would probably be on largely the same track with or without the mentor's involvement due to their inherent familial advantages. Based on my limited experiences I believe the mentoring relationship Ladd has put in place would be much more valuable to young men who do not have the fortunate home and economic opportunities Ladd has provided. This is no one's fault, however, as I previously noted.

So my conclusions about the concept of the Protestant Bar Mitzvah are: 1) it provides a wonderful base of expectations from which a respective young man can launch into young adulthood and therefore could be used in concept by any number of other situations; 2) the value of the mentoring aspects of the Protestant Bar Mitzvah can be muted by a strong familial base - in other words, the value may be greatest in those situations where a mentor is not available and a strong familial or economic base does not exist. Of course, this is the precise situation in which something resembling a Protestant Bar Mitzvah would be least likely to occur, so it would appear a chicken-or-egg situation would result. My thoughts on how to expand the Protestant Bar Mitzvah concept follow; however, outside a strong family environment the concept would require a highly organized and multi-decades effort complete with multiple personal commitments to succeed to the level it should. I believe the local church could have a role in something like an expanded Bar Mitzvah, but my experience, unfortunately, is that the local church does not have the stamina, attention, or desire to formally take on this responsibility, although I have freely said that men are not limited to their own families; we have a Scriptural obligation to offer help and hope to the "others" in society; and 3) all mentors need to be committed to maintaining a relationship with the mentees even with age and geographic distances. This is difficult for both parties but an intentional relationship is not accidental. It must be nurtured and pursued. Any mentor should acknowledge and accept this challenge before taking the mentor role.

Regarding the application of the Protestant Bar Mitzvah and the following mentor/mentee relationships, I have the following thought, hinted at previously: the local church or, probably faith-based, non-profit organizations could provide the resources, organization, time, and intentionality over years and decades to make a Protestant Bar Mitzvah and subsequent mentoring a successful enterprise. Since I view the Bar Mitzvah and mentoring efforts to both be required for program success, a sustained effort over years must be organized and maintained. This is difficult in any environment, but particularly outside an invested family. But for a program like this to be most effective it must be conducted outside an invested family, to be where the "lesser of these" is located. How to do this? A church could establish an annual Protestant Bar Mitzvah event where a certain number of young men could prepare for and move into the program, with volunteer mentors assigned to each child. On paper it appears possible; in fact, however, as I mentioned above, the sustained resources and volunteer commitment seems beyond almost every church's capability that I have seen. But how else to implement a program of this much potential value? I wish I could put a "finishing strong" presentation together which would extend this Protestant Bar Mitzvah concept to those most in need. Alas, I don't think I can.

But those children with the most to gain in our society could benefit, I am certain. I believe this idea should be explored. Ladd has provided a template.

Finally, Ladd must be commended for developing and implementing the Protestant Bar Mitzvah concept. I wish his young men well and that, when called upon, I will be up to the task of providing them Scripture-based guidance and assistance, as they were taught when preparing for the ceremony. To work with Ladd and his family has been a lifetime honor and one I have not taken lightly. My prayer is that these young men will reach their potential and remember the support of family and the infrastructure they provided as they move into adulthood.

ATTENDEE TUCKER BARRACLOUGH

Tucker is young man with a great head on his shoulders. He and Levi were friends at Midland Classical Academy. He has traveled the world with us. Rhonda and I think that this is a young man we would adopt in a moment if the need ever arose. We have enjoyed his eating dinner at our kitchen table, his laughing at the craziness in our home, and his growing through the years. His responses to my questions for attendees:

1) When I heard about a Protestant Bar Mitzvah, I thought:

I thought very little of it. I was too young to think about what it meant beyond being an excuse to spend more time with the people I loved. When I first heard of it, it had no name. I had been invited to a coming-of-age ceremony for my friend's older brother and I was delighted to go, despite knowing nothing of the actual event. While I recall thinking that the idea was very strange, I had not been exposed to the Jewish culture, and so I did not have a clear analogue in mind to compare it to; it was unique to me.

2) One of the things that stood out to me was how deeply meaningful the ceremony was to the Hoffman boys. I first witnessed this with Lincoln in the aftermath of his Bar Mitzvah. He was acutely aware that the expectations of him were greater now, that he had to act in a manner worthy his status as a man. Additionally, his defense of faith had strengthened his standing as a man of God; he knew that he was ready and able to give a reason for the hope that was in him, as we are called to be in Jesus.

I then saw this with Levi. His older brother had set a precedent of reverence for the process of the ceremony. I was with Levi throughout his preparation for the Bar Mitzvah. He felt pressure to perform well, but he was also excited for the event; beyond excitement for the measly few hours that constituted the event, he was excited for what it signified. Just like Lincoln, he was expected to act responsibly as a man. Levi knew this and yearned for that validation of his growth.

Lastly, I witnessed this with Legend. By the time Legend's Bar Mitzvah came around, the significance of the process had been well established. Watching his two brothers take on the growth signified by the process, Legend had good examples to follow and understand the gravity of what was being demonstrated.

3) One of the things that I had never considered was the massive preparation that went into the ceremony. Watching Lincoln's Bar Mitzvah, I was impressed by the display, but watching Levi's preparations, I gained a greater respect for the efforts involved. Levi's preparation caused him to carefully consider where he stood on several important matters of his faith in God; he was given the chance to consider these questions, make a decision on them, and fortify his heart, mind, and soul in his pursuit of God. I believe that the Hoffmans all

benefited from the exercise in responsible preparation that the Bar Mitzvah provided.

4) If I were planning this for one of my children or grandchildren, I would model it very closely after the three Protestant Bar Mitzvahs that I have observed. I would likely tailor the ceremony to the personal interests of my children or grandchildren. With the Hoffman boys, personalization was found largely in the music portion, with each boy playing a different selection of music on their instrument of choice. Being that I do not yet have any children, I cannot even begin to imagine what I would specifically change to suit them, except that I would like to see their personal interests made a part of the ceremony, whether they are musical or not.

5) If I could change anything about the process, I would change the defense of faith portion of the ceremony by adding a time wherein any guests may formulate and ask challenging questions for the young man to answer. I believe that questions from others outside of the immediate family, who may think and feel differently, would make the defense of faith a tougher, but more valuable exercise.

6) My final thoughts are that the Protestant Bar Mitzvah is a process and ceremony that is as valuable as it is unusual. I have been honored to watch all three Hoffman boys undergo the process and all three have been bettered by it. It stands as a marker of growth and responsibility, and is celebrated by a display of skill in apologetics and music. The metaphor of the passing of the baton and the gift of the ring symbolizes this newfound status within the family that is both desirable and beneficial.

ATTENDEE MARK LINDSEY

Mark Lindsey is my friend. He is my former pastor. He is a great man of God. I have learned from him. I have done ministry with him. I have served him. These are his responses to the questions about the Bar Mitzvah:

When I heard about a Protestant Bar Mitzvah, I thought what a wonderful idea! This is something which is desperately needed in preparing young men as followers of Christ to be the light of Christ in our darkened world.

One of the things that stood out to me was the intensity of study and preparation to complete the task by the young man. Also, the depth of Scripture study required to properly defend one's faith. This is not simply a memory exercise, but a lifestyle commitment.

One of the things I had never considered was providing a wide range of eternal influences, such as a variety of mentors. These trusted men/women will continue to mold the lives of their charges following the final "ceremony."

If I would change anything about the process, I would have the prospect share his weaknesses or challenges in his walk of faith. What in his spiritual journey needs growth? How has he handled real life conversations with his peers concerning spiritual matters? What is one area in which others can pray on his behalf?

A Protestant Bar Mitzvah has the potential to develop young men into warriors for Christ in their family, in their community, and in their school. This is the opportunity to build a strong foundation of faith which is lacking in many men of the church today.

ATTENDEE SHERRY LINDSEY

Mrs. Sherry is my dear friend, but I need to make a confession. I misspelled her name for many years - Sherri. Not sure how I got the original misspelling, but she never corrected me for years. As is evidence by this forgiveness, she has a heart of gold. Her responses:

1) When I heard about a Protestant Bar Mitzvah, I thought:
I really knew very little about what takes place in a Jewish Bar Mitzvah. If your readers are like me, they may need some education from a Jewish perspective and then relate that to what you've accomplished with your boys.

2) One of the things that stood out to me was:
It was all impressive!

3) One of the things that I had never considered was:
The whole idea is one I've never considered.

4) If you were planning this for one of your children or grandchildren, I would:
N/A

5) If I could change anything about the process, I would change:
NOTHING

6) My final thoughts:
Your family already does this, you live it day in and day out… I've been thinking about a family who wants to implement what you've done with their own kids. How, practically, could their kids be encouraged to use their answers to defend their faith in a way that is experiential and not just rote memory? Your family lives missionally, so defending faith is used as a way of life. I have no idea how you would encourage this. I was just thinking that missional experiences would help what a child studies to penetrate more deeply and then the Bar Mitzvah would be an overflow of experiences plus Scripture memory.

This is a tool that parents need to have in their hands to better equip their children for these last days that are ahead!

ATTENDEE JEAN HODGES

When I am on call at the hospital, I need to be within 15 minutes of the Emergency Room. When I began working in Henderson, Mrs. Jean allowed me to use an apartment behind her house as my roost, as our home is 30 minutes away in Carthage, Texas. She is a true blessing to me. She got to witness the last ceremony for the runt, Legend.

1) When I heard about a Protestant Bar Mitzvah, I thought:
I would love to see what a Bar Mitzvah was.

2) One of the things that stood out to me was:
It was so planned and was done with such love for Legend.

3) One of the things that I had never considered was:
That a dad and son were so close with love.

4) If you were planning this for one of your children or grandchildren, I would:
Pray for each one to be so strong in the Lord and mean each answer.

5) If I could change anything about the process, I would change:

It was the most beautiful and meaningful thing I have ever been invited to.

6) My final thoughts:

I felt very special to have been invented to the Bar Mitzvah. Dr. Hoffman and Legend were so very perfect in the questioning and the Biblical answers. Thank you so very much for inviting me to such a special event!

ATTENDEE DR. D. WARD

Dr. Ward is our former dentist when we lived in Big Spring. He has a great practice and is a man of God. He saw the first ceremony with Lincoln and provided his answers to my questions.

1) When I heard about a Protestant Bar Mitzvah, I thought:

This is a great opportunity for me to find out what happens at a Bar Mitzvah and to support the Hoffman family. I knew basically the purpose of a Bar Mitzvah, ushering in adulthood at a young age within the teachings of Judaism, or in this case Christianity.

2) One of the things that stood out to me was:

I was amazed at the preparation that went into your son's ceremony. Our girls did senior recitals, UIL competitions, etc, but the spiritual and scriptural preparation was awe inspiring.

3) One of the things that I had never considered was:

I had never considered how much a 13- or 14-year-old could contemplate, learn, and memorize to confirm their faith in their own mind and even defend the faith as I recall from your questioning him.

4) If you were planning this for one of your children or grandchildren, I would:

If planning a ceremony for a grandchild in our case I would start by discussing with their parents what we witnessed. It was an amazing afternoon. Certainly, their parents would be the most critical component of making this a possibility for our grandchildren.

5) If I could change anything about the process, I would change:

Since I have been to only one Bar Mitzvah, Christian or otherwise, so I have to assume that it was perfect!

6) My final thoughts:

When our daughters were growing up, they are both in their 30's, it was a different world to some degree. We had the kids in Bible Class almost every Sunday growing up. In our mostly conservative small town, we didn't think their faith would be potentially challenged until high school and college. Really, I didn't think till college, but during their high school years I was having discussions with them, usually in the car as I recall. I tried to prepare them for the likely challenges ahead for their faith, that they may be presented "facts" that would conflict with their view of the world. While I had no college professors, in the sciences or other subjects, who actively attacked the faith of their students, I advised them that they were around. Today, teachers attacking their faith can start in elementary school. I hope and pray not in our small town, but who knows. Since our grandkids are in the Houston area, it is certainly possible. Maintaining one's faith in our God the Father, God the Son, and God the Holy Spirit, is the most important lifelong endeavor any Christian can have. As parents and grandparents, we older Christians must recognize the battle for the very souls of our loved ones, and prepare them to engage the enemy at a very young age. Teachers and professors these days can't share their faith, but they can surely attack the faith of their students mostly without consequences. We must prepare them!

ATTENDEES ELAYNE AND ERNIE HANSON

The original version of this book was written in 2015, and I waited patiently till all of the boys had completed their ceremony. Thankfully, I provided a copy to some friends to review and provide feedback. The follow letter is from Elayne and Ernie Hanson:

We were honored and blessed to attend Lincoln's Protestant Christian Bar Mitzvah and doubly honored to get to relive it through Ladd's journal. I hope God allows a way for this to be published. I feel it will open up vistas for parents who are trying to find a way to prepare their children to believing adults - their profession of faith and obedience as servants of our Lord.

You asked be to write down or thought and feelings about the event, but I can't help including my thoughts about the journal. It was wonderful. The poetry of Ebenezer is beautiful, and how "thus far the Lord has helped us' is the cornerstone and draws focus to each facet of the process. Ladd's humility and deference to the wisdom of God and giving Him the glory was obvious. His humor was spot on (loved the portable ashtray and Momma-Nut's dream of a baby girl). His engaging method of writing flowed so easily. I read portions of it to Ernie as we drove around town and laughed together. When you publish, I hope you include an After Word from Lincoln. It was mentioned that he is a budding author, so what better way of getting some practice. I'd like to know how he felt throughout the process and in the days leading up to the actual event and if he feels changed and how after the occasion (besides the laundry, that is).

I want to include this although I couldn't really find a good place to put it. From the early pages of the journal, I was hooked when I read, "You should expect a continual haze of uncertainty to be present in your child. There will never be a moment when they are expected to pick up the gauntlet and to accept the challenge of adult living." The term "arrested development" came to my mind. How many grown adults walk around in a state of arrested development. My own life as a teenage and my husband as well found us making adult decisions too early when we did not have the emotional or spiritual maturity to do so. Yes, you can survive through life like that but at some point, there will be a crisis. It may be a crisis of faith or you can find yourself destroying other people. You will live confused and muddled and never really know where you are going. You can look back at 40-50-60 years old and realize that you have the emotional maturity of a 10-year-old. Praise God who loves us as we are. With Lincoln being told from a very early age that he would be a man, it became his reality and he faces a more certain future.

The occasion itself: I began to see the importance of the event when you texted me his photo in the tux and remember thinking, "he already looks grown up!" It was one more aspect of your careful thought of the specialness of this occasion because donning the formal attire had to change the way he walked, talked, thought, and prepared for the big day. I think 16 years old is a good age to do this because it is before the distractions of college applications and graduation and it's a tall order for someone younger but as Ladd mentioned in the journal, this is a judgment for each individual case. The affair itself was classy, but not ostentatious. The music and Lincoln's commentary was very nice, especially for those of us with little background knowledge in music.

His defense of faith was amazing and the Scriptures carefully chosen. I was glad to be able to read them again in the journal so I could follow the stages of ways we all need to defend our faith. I've read some of the books that were part of Lincoln's training - some of it is heavy stuff - but Lincoln has an obvious intelligence and capacity for comprehending. Ladd's own testimony before the passing of the baton was essential and the way he honored the matriarchs was touching.

The choice of questions, especially "What are your fears and What are you hopes?" I felt were inspired by God to receptive, loving and thoughtful parents. How many of us can put into words to those things and Lincoln acknowledging them will make him stronger, more centered and to know himself. These are questions that he should evaluate intermittently throughout various stages of his life. I urge you to ask him again when you sense hesitation in his life. Giving them voice will relieve the pressure.

The magnitude of Lincoln's commitment and preparation was awesome as well as your commitment. My husband's comment was what an awesome gift you have given your son. I pray he and the other boys will continue the legacy for their children. I pray also that other parents will take on this challenge. It gives

Ernie and I hope in the next generation and to quote Ladd, "The story is not always about this generation."

We drove home that night in a state of God's grace and revived faith. When I read about the Saturday morning session, I could imagine how the Holy Spirit must have filled the room. My God bless your work and show you that you have planted this young man in fertile soil, deeply rooted and producing much fruit.

For Lincoln, I would repeat something a wise woman told me: Give your testimonies repeatedly as they unfold in the years to come as witness to God's miracles in your life. Tell them often so they remain forefront in your mind and fresh as the day you experienced God's great love.

Elayne and Ernie Hanson
May 2015

When I called to ask them permission to use this letter, they had almost forgotten about the letter. We had a great visit. These type of events grow out our your effort to see this process to the end.

POSTLUDE

Thank you for taking the time to walk the road of a Protestant Bar Mitzvah with us. My hope is that other young boys and girls will be challenged to reach higher, to stand taller, and to grow spiritually. It would be great to one day hear about the ceremonies that were created to celebrate adulthood in those coming behind us.

If you need to reach me, my cell phone is actually 832-971-3611. My phone will not recognize unknown callers, but leave a message and I will do my best to get back with you. If I am operating, it may be a while.

Email: lchoffmanmd@sbcglobal.net

Come visit:
Www.stillwood.estate

ABOUT THE AUTHOR

Ladd C. Hoffman MD, MBA, MHA was born in Houston, Texas. He was in the last graduating class of Spring Branch High School. He got a math degree from Louisiana State University in Shreveport. After briefly teaching, he was accepted into medical school and graduated (MD) from Louisiana State University Health Sciences Center in Shreveport. He finished a Masters of Business Administration (MBA) at night while in medical school. He threw in a Masters of Health care Administration (MHA) to take up the time at night while on call at the hospital. He is a general surgeon who does endoscopy as well.

    He has been married to Rhonda for 28 years. He does not hunt, does not fish, does not golf, and is basically a boring person. He has one patent. He has authored some poetry. He loves his sons (all 5 of them!). He trades stocks.

www.ingramcontent.com/pod-product-compliance
Lightning Source LLC
Chambersburg PA
CBHW070453100426

42743CB00010B/1602